BEST API DEVELOPMENT
PRACTICES FOR BEGINNERS

Master The Fundamentals Of Modern API Development With Ease

KRISTINE ELLIS

Introduction   1

  Why This Book?   1

  Who This Book is For   2

  How to Get the Most Out of This Book   3

    1. Follow Along With the Examples   3

    2. Work on the Mini Projects   3

    3. Take On the Challenges   4

    4. Refer to the Diagrams and Flowcharts   4

    5. Leverage the Free Resources   4

    6. Stay Consistent   4

  Free Resources and Code Repository Access   5

    1. Complete Source Code   5

    2. Postman Collections   5

    3. API Design Templates   5

    4. Interview Preparation Guide   6

  Final Thoughts Before We Begin   6

Chapter 1: Understanding APIs — The Backbone of Modern Software   7

  1.1 What is an API?   7

  1.2 How APIs Power the Apps You Use Every Day   8

    1. Social Media Applications   8

    2. Weather Applications   9

    3. E-commerce Websites   9

    4. Travel and Booking Services   10

    5. Banking and Financial Services   10

  1.3 Types of APIs: REST, GraphQL, SOAP (Brief Introduction)   11

    1. REST (Representational State Transfer)   11

    2. GraphQL   12

    3. SOAP (Simple Object Access Protocol)   13

    Quick Comparison: 14

  1.4 Why Learning API Development is a Game Changer   14

    1. APIs Are the Foundation of Modern Apps   14

    2. APIs Open Up Endless Opportunities for Integration   15

    3. APIs Are the Future of Business   15

    4. API Skills Future-Proof Your Career   16

    5. APIs Empower Innovation   16

  1.5 API Development: Essential Skills and Career Advantages   17

1. Core Technical Skills You Gain	17
2. Career Advantages of API Development Skills	19
Chapter 2: The Basics of Web Communication	**22**
2.1 How the Internet and Web Requests Work	22
What Happens When You Access a Website?	22
Clients and Servers	23
The Role of Protocols	23
2.2 HTTP Protocol Essentials	24
Structure of an HTTP Request	24
Structure of an HTTP Response	25
Important HTTP Status Codes	26
2.3 HTTP Methods: GET, POST, PUT, PATCH, DELETE	26
1. GET	27
2. POST	27
3. PUT	28
4. PATCH	29
5. DELETE	30
Summary Table of HTTP Methods:	31
2.4 Status Codes: 200s, 400s, 500s Explained	31
1. 200s: Success Codes	31
2. 400s: Client Error Codes	32
3. 500s: Server Error Codes	33
Why Proper Status Codes Matter	34
2.5 Anatomy of a Web API Request and Response	34
The API Request Structure	35
The API Response Structure	36
A Simple Example: Full Request-Response	37
Chapter 3: Introduction to REST API Principles	**39**
3.1 What Makes an API RESTful?	39
1. Statelessness	39
2. Uniform Interface	40
3. Resource-Based	40
4. Client-Server Separation	41
5. Representation of Resources	41
6. Stateless Communication over HTTP	41
In Summary:	42
3.2 Resources, Endpoints, and Methods	42

1. Resources   42

2. Endpoints   43

3. Methods   44

3.3 Understanding CRUD Operations   45

1. Create (POST)   45

2. Read (GET)   46

3. Update (PUT or PATCH)   47

4. Delete (DELETE)   48

CRUD Operations Summary: 49

3.4 Statelessness, Cacheability, and Layered Systems   49

Statelessness   49

Cacheability   50

Layered Systems   51

3.5 REST API Design Best Practices   52

1. Use Nouns, Not Verbs, in Endpoints   53

2. Keep URLs Simple and Predictable   53

3. Use HTTP Status Codes Properly   54

4. Support Filtering, Sorting, and Pagination   54

5. Design Error Responses Clearly   55

6. Version Your API   55

7. Secure Sensitive Endpoints   56

8. Document Your API   56

Chapter 4: Understanding Data Formats — JSON, XML, and Beyond   **57**

4.1 Why JSON Dominates API Communication   57

1. Simplicity and Readability   57

2. Native Compatibility with JavaScript   58

3. Lightweight and Efficient   58

4. Language-Agnostic   59

5. Structured Yet Flexible   59

6. Standardized and Evolving   59

Real-World Examples   60

In Summary   60

4.2 Working with JSON Objects and Arrays   61

JSON Objects   61

JSON Arrays   63

Nesting Objects and Arrays   65

JSON Rules You Must Follow   66

Common Mistakes | 67
4.3 Brief Overview: XML, YAML, and When They Matter | 68
XML (eXtensible Markup Language) | 68
YAML (YAML Ain't Markup Language) | 70
Quick Comparison Table | 71
Practical Advice for API Developers | 71
4.4 Handling Data Serialization and Parsing | 71
What is Serialization? | 72
What is Parsing? | 73
Why Serialization and Parsing Matter in API Development | 74
Common Pitfalls to Avoid | 75
Bonus Tip: Automated Serialization and Parsing | 75
Chapter 5: Designing Great APIs That Developers Love | **77**
5.1 The Art of Resource Naming | 77
General Principles for Naming Resources | 77
Quick Checklist for Resource Naming | 81
5.2 Organizing Routes and URL Structures | 81
Organizing by Resource Hierarchy | 82
Use Nesting When It Makes Sense (But Don't Overdo It) | 82
Flat Structure for Top-Level Resources | 83
Use Query Parameters for Filtering and Actions | 83
Standard Action Endpoints | 84
Summary: API Routing Golden Rules | 84
5.3 API Versioning Strategies | 85
What is API Versioning? | 85
Why Version Your API? | 85
Common API Versioning Strategies | 86
1. URI Versioning (Recommended for Beginners) | 86
2. Header Versioning | 87
3. Query Parameter Versioning | 88
Best Practices for Versioning | 88
5.4 Error Handling and Standardized Responses | 89
The Importance of Good Error Responses | 89
Key Components of a Good Error Response | 90
Standardizing Error Format Across Your API | 91
Using the Right Status Codes for Errors | 92
Helpful Tips for Error Handling | 92

5.5 Writing Clear and Helpful API Documentation   93

     Why Great Documentation Matters   93

     Essential Sections of Good API Documentation   94

     Best Practices for API Documentation   97

     Tools to Help Write and Maintain API Docs   98

Chapter 6: Your First API — A Practical Guide   **99**

     6.1 Setting Up Your Development Environment   99

     Tools You Need   99

     Setting Up Your Machine   100

     Final Quick Checklist   101

     6.2 Choosing Your First Tech Stack (Python Flask or Node.js Express)   102

     Option 1: Python Flask   102

     Option 2: Node.js Express   103

     How to Decide?   104

     6.3 Building Your First Simple REST API (Step-by-Step)   104

     Step 1: Initialize Your Project   104

     Step 2: Set Up Your API Server   105

     Step 3: Run Your API   107

     Step 4: Test Your API   107

     Step 5: Celebrate (You Deserve It)   109

     6.4 Testing Locally with Postman or Curl   109

     Testing with Postman   109

         Step 1: Install Postman   110

         Step 2: Sending a Simple GET Request   110

         Step 3: Sending a POST Request   111

         Step 4: Checking Errors   112

     Testing with Curl (Command Line)   112

     Why Test Locally Before Deploying?   113

     6.5 Common Mistakes to Avoid in Your First API   114

     1. Not Using Proper HTTP Status Codes   114

     2. Forgetting to Validate Incoming Data   114

     3. Ignoring Error Handling   116

     4. Hardcoding Data Without Future Consideration   117

     5. Not Structuring Project Files Properly   117

     6. Forgetting About Security   118

Chapter 7: Testing and Debugging Your API Like a Pro   **119**

     7.1 Introduction to API Testing Tools (Postman, Thunder Client)   119

Postman: The Industry Standard   119

Thunder Client: Lightweight and Fast   120

Which Tool Should You Use?   121

Tip:
Use Thunder Client for quick local development testing, and Postman when you
need full testing suites, API docs, or environment switching.   121

7.2 Writing Basic Test Cases for Your Endpoints   121

What Should a Basic API Test Cover?   122

Example: Testing a POST /users Endpoint   122

How to Write a Basic Test in Postman   123

7.3 Automating API Testing with Scripts   124

Postman Collection Runner   124

Writing Multiple Assertions   125

Bonus Tip: Environment Variables   125

7.4 Debugging Common API Issues   126

1. 404 Not Found   126

2. 400 Bad Request   126

3. 401 Unauthorized   127

4. 500 Internal Server Error   127

5. Incorrect Data Returned   128

Chapter 8: Securing Your API   **130**

8.1 Why API Security Matters   130

Real-World Risks of Poor API Security   130

8.2 Introduction to API Keys and Basic Authentication   131

API Keys   131

Basic Authentication   132

8.3 Understanding Tokens and JWT (Beginner-Friendly)   133

What is a Token?   134

What is a JWT (JSON Web Token)?   134

8.4 Rate Limiting: Protecting Your API from Abuse   135

Why Rate Limiting Matters   136

How Rate Limiting Works   136

Implementing Rate Limiting (Overview)   137

8.5 CORS, HTTPS, and Basic Security Configurations   137

CORS (Cross-Origin Resource Sharing)   137

HTTPS: Always Secure the Transport   139

Other Basic Security Tips   139

Chapter 9: Pagination, Filtering, and Sorting   **140**

9.1 Handling Large Data Sets Efficiently 140
Why You Should Never Return Everything at Once 141
9.2 Designing Pagination (Offset, Cursor-Based) 141
Offset-Based Pagination 141
Cursor-Based Pagination 142
How to Decide? 143
Tip:
Start simple (offset) but learn cursor-based techniques early — they're essential for scalable APIs. 144
9.3 Implementing Filtering and Search Parameters 144
Common Filtering Techniques 144
Example of a Filtered Request 144
Best Practices for Filtering 145
Implementing Search 145
9.4 Sorting API Responses Properly 145
How to Allow Sorting in Your API 146
Default Sort Orders 146
Sorting Best Practices 147
Combining Pagination + Filtering + Sorting 147
Chapter 10: API Performance and Caching Essentials **148**
10.1 Why Performance Matters 148
How API Performance Impacts Real-World Applications 148
What "Good Performance" Means for APIs 149
Key Factors Affecting API Performance 149
10.2 Introduction to Caching Techniques (Client-side and Server-side) 150
Types of Caching 150
1. Client-Side Caching 150
2. Server-Side Caching 151
Caching Strategy Tips 152
10.3 Adding Simple Caching to Your APIs 152
1. Setting Cache-Control Headers (Client-Side) 152
2. Adding Simple In-Memory Server Caching 153
3. Using Real Cache Engines (Next Level) 154
Caching Best Practices 154
10.4 Monitoring API Performance 154
Why Monitor API Performance? 155
Key Metrics to Monitor 155
How to Monitor Your APIs 155

1. Manual Monitoring (During Development) 155
2. Basic Logging 156
3. Using Professional Monitoring Tools 157
Chapter 11: Documentation and Publishing Best Practices **158**
11.1 Introduction to OpenAPI and Swagger 158
What is OpenAPI? 158
Why OpenAPI Matters 159
What is Swagger? 159
11.2 Documenting Your API with Swagger UI 160
Step 1: Create Your OpenAPI Specification 160
Step 2: Install Swagger UI 162
Step 3: Customize and Polish 163
11.3 Hosting Your API Documentation Online 164
Option 1: Host Swagger UI Yourself 164
Option 2: Use SwaggerHub 164
Option 3: Publish Static Docs 165
Best Practices for Public API Documentation 165
11.4 How to Publish and Share Your API on GitHub 166
Step 1: Prepare Your Repository 166
Step 2: Push to GitHub 166
Step 3: Enable GitHub Pages (Optional) 167
Bonus: Badges and Enhancements 167
Chapter 12: Mini Project — Simple Blog Post API **168**
12.1 Project Setup and Requirements 168
What We Will Build 168
Technologies You Can Use 169
Project Structure 169
Key Requirements 169
12.2 Building CRUD Endpoints for Posts 170
Create a New Post — POST /posts 170
Get All Posts — GET /posts 171
Get a Single Post by ID — GET /posts/:id 172
Update a Post — PUT /posts/:id 172
Delete a Post — DELETE /posts/:id 173
Sample In-Memory Data Storage 173
12.3 Adding Simple Authentication for Admin Users 174
Simple Authentication Logic 174

Protecting Routes (Flask Example)   174
Protecting Routes (Express Example)   175
Good Practices   175
12.4 Testing and Documenting the Blog API   175
Testing the Blog API (Manual)   175
Documenting the Blog API   176
Chapter 13: Mini Project — Weather Information API   **179**
13.1 Setting Up Third-Party Weather API Integration   179
Choosing a Weather API Provider   179
Setting Up Your Weather API Account   180
How Weather API Calls Work   180
13.2 Creating Endpoints for Weather Queries   181
Project Structure   181
Building the Endpoints   182
1. Current Weather Endpoint   182
2. Forecast Endpoint (Optional Advanced)   182
Example API Response (Your API)   182
Example Weather Service Module   183
13.3 Handling API Keys Securely   184
How to Handle API Keys Properly   184
Good Practice Example   185
13.4 Adding City-Based Filtering and Forecast Feature   186
City-Based Filtering (Already Built-In)   186
Adding Forecast Feature   186
Building a /forecast Endpoint   186
Chapter 14: Mini Project — User Registration and Login API   **188**
14.1 Building Secure User Registration   188
What We Will Build   188
Required Data for Users   189
Project Structure Overview   189
Basic Workflow   189
Registration Endpoint (POST /register)   190
14.2 Hashing Passwords for Safe Storage   191
What is Password Hashing?   191
How to Hash Passwords   192
How to Verify Passwords During Login   192
Good Hashing Practices   193

14.3 Login with Token-Based Authentication (JWT)   193

    Why Use JWTs?   193

    Login Endpoint (POST /login)   193

    Server Logic   194

    Example JWT Payload   194

    How to Generate JWTs   195

    Response Example   195

14.4 Refresh Tokens and Session Management (Intro Level)   196

    What is a Refresh Token?   196

    Refresh Token Flow   196

    Example /refresh Endpoint   197

    Simple Implementation Ideas   197

Chapter 15: A Beginner's Glimpse into GraphQL and Modern Trends   **198**

15.1 What is GraphQL? Why It Matters   198

    What is GraphQL?   198

    A Simple GraphQL Example   198

    Why GraphQL Matters   200

15.2 Key Differences Between REST and GraphQL   200

15.3 When to Use REST vs When to Explore GraphQL   201

    When to Use REST   201

    When to Consider GraphQL   201

15.4 Brief Overview of Serverless APIs (AWS Lambda Example)   202

    What is Serverless?   202

    How Serverless APIs Work   203

    Simple Example: AWS Lambda + API Gateway   203

    Advantages of Serverless APIs   204

    Limitations to Be Aware Of   204

Chapter 16: Career Tips for Aspiring API Developers   **205**

16.1 How to Showcase API Skills on Your Resume   205

    1. Focus on Outcomes, Not Just Tools   205

    2. Highlight Real Projects   205

    3. Use Proper Technical Terminology   206

    4. Resume Section Structure   207

16.2 GitHub: Your Best API Portfolio Platform   207

    Why GitHub Matters for API Developers   207

    Best Practices for an API-Focused GitHub   208

      1. Upload Your Projects   208

2. Write Good README Files   208
3. Use Meaningful Commit Messages   209
4. Showcase Testing and Documentation   209
Bonus: Create a GitHub Portfolio Page   210
16.3 Preparing for API Development Interview Questions   210
Common API Interview Topics   210
1. API Design Questions   210
2. HTTP Concepts   210
3. Authentication and Security   211
4. Performance and Scaling   211
Tips for API Interviews   211
16.4 Next Steps: Moving to Intermediate and Advanced API Development 212
1. Learn Advanced API Security   212
2. Deepen Your Understanding of Databases   212
3. Build Full-Stack Applications   213
4. Learn API Gateway and Microservices Architecture   213
5. Deploy APIs Like a Pro   213
APPENDICES   **215**
Appendix A: API Development Glossary   **215**
API (Application Programming Interface)   215
REST (Representational State Transfer)   215
CRUD   215
Endpoint   215
HTTP Methods   215
Status Code   216
JSON (JavaScript Object Notation)   216
JWT (JSON Web Token)   216
OpenAPI Specification   216
Swagger   216
Authentication vs Authorization   217
Token-Based Authentication   217
Rate Limiting   217
CORS (Cross-Origin Resource Sharing)   217
Serverless   217
Appendix B: Common API Interview Questions and Answers   **217**
1. What is REST API?   217
2. What are the main HTTP methods used in APIs?   218

3. What is the difference between PUT and PATCH? 218

4. What is an Idempotent Method? 218

5. What is JWT? How does it work? 218

6. What is Rate Limiting? 219

7. How do you secure an API? 219

8. What's the difference between Authentication and Authorization? 219

9. What is CORS and why is it important? 219

10. What is an API Gateway? 219

Appendix C: Free Tools and Resources for API Developers **220**

Tools for API Development 220

Hosting and Deployment 220

Learning Platforms 220

API Design and Documentation Tools 220

Communities and Forums 221

Appendix D: Bonus Material Access Guide **221**

1. Source Code Repositories 221

2. API Starter Templates 221

3. Postman Collections 222

4. OpenAPI Specs and Swagger Docs 222

How to Access 222

Introduction

Why This Book?

In today's fast-evolving technological landscape, APIs are the invisible bridges that connect software systems, devices, and people. They are everywhere—whether you are booking a flight, checking the weather on your smartphone, sharing a post on social media, or making an online payment. Behind the scenes, APIs are quietly enabling seamless communication between countless services, shaping the way we interact with technology every day.

Yet, for beginners stepping into the world of programming or backend development, the concept of API development often seems intimidating, complex, or reserved only for the so-called "advanced" developers. Many resources out there either drown readers in jargon or assume a background in sophisticated software engineering principles. As a result, countless beginners feel discouraged before they even write their first line of API code.

This book was born out of the need to fill that gap.

"Best API Development Practices for Beginners: Master the Fundamentals of Modern API Development with Ease" is designed to provide an accessible, structured, and practical guide for those who are new to API development. It focuses not only on the "how" but also on the "why," ensuring that readers develop a solid conceptual foundation while gaining hands-on skills they can apply immediately. Every explanation, project, and example in this book is crafted with a beginner's mindset in mind—clear, relatable, and actionable.

We understand that you do not want a dry, textbook-like experience filled with abstract theories. You want to build real APIs. You want to understand the purpose behind each decision. You want to avoid common beginner mistakes, and you want to feel confident enough to integrate APIs into real-world applications or even create APIs that others can use. Most importantly, you want a book that treats you as a capable learner, not as someone who needs to be overwhelmed by unnecessary complexity.

This book is your companion in that journey. It promises to walk you through every step, every building block, and every important principle needed to master the fundamentals of modern API development. From understanding simple request-response cycles to securing your APIs, from building a basic CRUD service to designing and documenting professional-grade APIs, this book covers it all — without making you feel lost or left behind.

If you have been searching for a guide that demystifies API development while empowering you to build confidently, you are holding it in your hands right now.

Welcome. Your journey toward mastering APIs begins here.

Who This Book is For

This book is crafted specifically for individuals who want to learn API development from the ground up. It does not assume that you are already an experienced backend developer or that you are comfortable with advanced server-side concepts. Instead, it meets you exactly where you are — whether you are taking your first steps into coding or looking to bridge a gap in your existing skills.

You will find this book perfect if you are:

- **A Complete Beginner to Backend Development:** If you know basic programming concepts (variables, loops, functions) but have never built a server or an API, this book will gently introduce you to the world of APIs, web protocols, and backend services.

- **A Frontend Developer Expanding Your Skills:** If you are a frontend web or mobile developer who consumes APIs but wants to learn how they are built, this book will help you understand the server side, giving you full-stack development confidence.

- **A Mobile App Developer Needing Custom APIs:** Whether you are building iOS or Android apps, having control over your backend data through your own APIs can massively boost your project capabilities.

- **A Computer Science Student Seeking Practical Knowledge:** Academic courses often focus on theory. This book focuses on real-world application, helping you turn theoretical understanding into tangible skills.

- **A No-Code or Low-Code Enthusiast Curious About APIs:** Even if you use platforms like Zapier, Bubble, or others, understanding APIs will supercharge your ability to connect services and extend functionality beyond basic options.

- **A Junior Software Engineer Looking to Strengthen Fundamentals:** If you are already working in tech but feel gaps in your API knowledge, this book will reinforce best practices and equip you for more complex projects ahead.

No matter your background, if you have the willingness to learn, this book is designed for you. It assumes no prior experience with API development, no previous knowledge of frameworks like Flask or Express, and no understanding of protocols like HTTP beyond what we will cover together.

You do not need to be an expert to start. You just need to be willing to learn step-by-step, try out the projects, and ask questions along the way. If you are ready to do that, then this book will not only teach you API development — it will empower you to master it.

How to Get the Most Out of This Book

Learning a technical skill is much like learning a new language or sport: passive reading is not enough. Mastery comes through doing. That is why this book is deliberately structured to blend reading, hands-on practice, and active engagement.

To truly maximize your learning, here's how you should approach the journey:

1. Follow Along With the Examples

This book is filled with practical examples that you should not just read but actually build on your computer. Typing the code out yourself — rather than copy-pasting — will help reinforce patterns, logic, and syntax in a way that passive reading never could.

You will understand not just *what* the code is doing, but *why* it is structured that way.

2. Work on the Mini Projects

Starting from the middle chapters, we will build real mini-projects together: from a simple blog API to a weather information API to a secure login system. These projects are critical. They connect the concepts you learn to tangible outcomes. Set aside time to complete each one fully before moving on.

Even if the project seems simple, completing it properly — including testing, securing, and documenting it — will mirror real-world development far more than you might expect.

3. Take On the Challenges

At the end of most chapters, you will find small challenges or exercises designed to stretch your understanding a little further. Try to solve them before looking at hints or moving forward. Treat them as opportunities to test yourself without judgment.

Mistakes are part of the process. Struggle a little — and you will grow a lot.

4. Refer to the Diagrams and Flowcharts

Whenever you feel overwhelmed by new terminology or processes (like request/response cycles or authentication flows), take a step back and study the diagrams provided. Visual learning can break down even the most complex topics into digestible, understandable chunks.

We included these visuals intentionally — because sometimes seeing something is faster and clearer than reading three paragraphs about it.

5. Leverage the Free Resources

Throughout the book, you will be directed to download source code, templates, and examples from the official code repository. Use these resources actively. Examine how the sample solutions are structured, compare them to your own work, and even modify them to experiment and learn further.

Your learning should not stop when the chapter ends — it should extend into tinkering and building beyond the examples.

6. Stay Consistent

The biggest pitfall for learners is inconsistency. If possible, commit to short, focused learning sessions daily or every other day, even if it is just one section or one example at a time. Consistency compounds understanding in powerful ways.

If you find yourself losing momentum, jump to a mini project for a motivational boost. Building something real is the fastest way to rekindle excitement and purpose.

Remember, this is not a race. It is a journey of building a skill that will pay you back in projects, opportunities, and professional growth for years to come.

Free Resources and Code Repository Access

To enhance your experience and save you from typing lengthy blocks of code, we have prepared a dedicated code repository and additional bonus materials. These resources are designed to make your learning more interactive, practical, and efficient.

Here is what you will have access to:

1. Complete Source Code

Every project, every chapter example, and even every minor snippet discussed in the book is available in organized folders inside the GitHub repository. This way, you can cross-reference your code, check your progress, or troubleshoot errors efficiently.

You will also find multiple versions of some projects — initial versions, intermediate improvements, and final versions — to help you understand the iterative nature of real-world development.

2. Postman Collections

All APIs we build will have ready-to-import Postman collections. Instead of manually creating requests, you can quickly load them into Postman and start testing right away, saving time and minimizing errors.

If you are new to Postman, don't worry — we will walk through how to use it step-by-step.

3. API Design Templates

We have included downloadable templates for designing your APIs: endpoint planning sheets, versioning plans, documentation outlines, and error response formats. These templates mirror professional development workflows and will save you countless hours in real-world projects.

You can use them for your learning or adapt them later for freelance work, hackathons, personal projects, or job assignments.

4. Interview Preparation Guide

As a bonus, you will find a PDF booklet with curated API interview questions and best-practice answers. These are common questions for entry-level and junior positions related to API development and will prepare you to speak confidently about your skills.

It includes behavioral questions, technical explanations, and tips on how to demonstrate your hands-on API knowledge during interviews.

Final Thoughts Before We Begin

This book is more than just a tutorial. It is a mentorship experience designed to unlock your full potential as a developer. By the end of this journey, you will not only know how to build modern, scalable, and secure APIs — you will have real confidence, real projects to show, and a real understanding of how professional API development works.

Take a breath, clear your mind, and get ready.
 Your hands-on, beginner-friendly journey into the world of APIs starts now.

Let's build something amazing together.

Chapter 1: Understanding APIs — The Backbone of Modern Software

1.1 What is an API?

At its core, an **API** — short for **Application Programming Interface** — is a set of rules that allows two software applications to talk to each other. Think of it as a messenger that delivers your request to a system and then returns the system's response back to you.

Imagine walking into a restaurant. You sit at a table, look at the menu, and place an order with the waiter. The kitchen prepares your food based on your order, and the waiter brings it back to your table. In this scenario, the waiter is the API. You, the customer, don't go into the kitchen, nor do you prepare the meal yourself — you simply communicate your need through a defined process (the menu and order system), and the service (the kitchen) fulfills it.

This analogy captures the essence of APIs. They **abstract the complexity** of the system behind them, **exposing only the necessary parts** needed for interaction, and **manage communication** efficiently and securely.

APIs are everywhere today — whenever you interact with a website, mobile app, or connected device, an API is likely handling the behind-the-scenes work that makes everything feel seamless.

At a technical level, an API defines a contract. It tells the client (the application making the request) what endpoints are available, what parameters are expected, and what the returned data will look like. By following this contract, different software components — even those written in different languages or running on different platforms — can work together harmoniously.

Without APIs, every software application would have to reinvent the wheel for every interaction, leading to chaos, inefficiency, and extremely limited functionality. APIs **standardize** these interactions, making innovation, scalability, and integration possible at the scale we experience today.

An API can:

- Fetch information from a database,

- Trigger a remote service,

- Send data for storage or processing,

- Authenticate users,

- Facilitate communication between microservices,

- Enable payment transactions, and much more.

Ultimately, APIs are the bridges connecting the vast, interconnected world of digital services — and understanding how they work is an essential skill for any modern developer.

1.2 How APIs Power the Apps You Use Every Day

You may not realize it, but nearly every interaction you have with modern technology involves APIs at some level. APIs are the invisible engines that quietly power the convenience and functionality you enjoy daily.

Let's explore some familiar examples.

1. Social Media Applications

When you open a social media app like Instagram, Twitter, or TikTok, APIs are at work in the background:

- Retrieving your latest feed posts,

- Sending your new photo upload to the server,

- Fetching notifications,

- Displaying trending hashtags,

- Logging you in securely.

Each of these actions relies on an API to communicate between your mobile device and the platform's backend servers. Without APIs efficiently carrying your requests back and forth, social media as you know it wouldn't exist.

2. Weather Applications

Think about the last time you checked the weather on your phone. Your weather app didn't calculate the weather conditions itself — it likely called a **third-party weather API** that aggregates data from various meteorological sources.

With a single API request, your app fetches:

- Current temperature,

- Forecasts,

- Wind speeds,

- UV index,

- Weather alerts.

This allows a small app to display comprehensive global weather information without building and maintaining its own network of weather stations.

3. E-commerce Websites

When you browse an online store like Amazon, Shopify sites, or eBay, APIs handle:

- Product searches,

- Pricing details,

- Shopping cart management,

- Payment processing through services like PayPal or Stripe,

- Shipment tracking.

An online purchase can involve multiple APIs working together, seamlessly linking inventory systems, payment gateways, and shipping providers behind the scenes — all while providing you a smooth customer experience.

4. Travel and Booking Services

Booking a flight, hotel, or rental car today usually involves pulling data from various sources:

- Flight schedules from airlines,

- Room availability from hotels,

- Car rental offers from fleets.

APIs aggregate this information in real time, allowing you to compare options, reserve your choice, and receive confirmations instantly. Without APIs, such multi-provider coordination would be painfully slow, if possible at all.

5. Banking and Financial Services

Modern banking apps allow you to:

- Check your balance,

- Pay bills,

- Transfer funds,

- Receive payment notifications.

All of these operations rely on secure APIs connecting your app to bank servers. Increasingly, "Open Banking" initiatives use standardized APIs to allow third-party apps to connect safely to your bank account — letting you manage your finances more flexibly than ever before.

In short, **APIs are the foundation** upon which the digital world is built. They make it possible for apps, platforms, and services to collaborate, share data, and deliver richer user experiences. Without APIs, the vast interconnected world of modern technology would be isolated, fragmented, and nowhere near as powerful as it is today.

By mastering API development, you are not just learning another programming skill — you are learning how to **build the connections that empower the digital future**.

1.3 Types of APIs: REST, GraphQL, SOAP (Brief Introduction)

As you venture deeper into API development, you'll quickly discover that not all APIs are built the same way. Different types of APIs have emerged over time, each suited to different needs, philosophies, and system architectures.

Let's take a closer look at three major API types you should be familiar with as a beginner: **REST**, **GraphQL**, and **SOAP**.

1. REST (Representational State Transfer)

REST is by far the most common and widely adopted API architectural style today, especially for web and mobile applications.

Key Characteristics of REST APIs:

- **Stateless:** Each request from the client to the server must contain all the information needed to understand and process it. The server does not store client session information.

- **Resource-Oriented:** REST treats data and functionality as resources that can be accessed using standard HTTP methods like GET, POST, PUT, DELETE.

- **Simple URLs:** RESTful APIs use clear, hierarchical URL structures that represent resources (e.g., /users/123/orders/456).

- **Flexible Data Formats:** Though JSON is the dominant format today, REST APIs can technically work with XML, YAML, or other formats.

Example:

Imagine a service providing book data:

- GET /books → Retrieve all books.

- GET /books/42 → Retrieve a specific book.

- POST /books → Add a new book.

- PUT /books/42 → Update a specific book.

- DELETE /books/42 → Delete a book.

REST is loved for its simplicity, scalability, and widespread adoption. It's beginner-friendly, and this book focuses heavily on helping you master REST fundamentals first.

2. GraphQL

GraphQL is a newer alternative to REST, created by Facebook in 2012 and open-sourced in 2015.

Key Characteristics of GraphQL:

- **Single Endpoint:** Instead of multiple endpoints like REST, a GraphQL API typically has a single /graphql endpoint.

- **Client-Driven Queries:** Clients specify exactly what data they need in a structured query format, and the server responds with only that data.

- **Efficient Data Fetching:** It minimizes over-fetching (getting more data than needed) and under-fetching (getting less data than needed).

Example:

A client could request:

```graphql
graphql
CopyEdit
{
  user(id: "123") {
    name
    email
    orders {
      id
      total
    }
  }
}
```

And receive precisely that information — no more, no less.

GraphQL shines when applications need highly dynamic queries, like in complex web dashboards or mobile apps needing to minimize data usage. However, it is a bit more complex to set up than REST and introduces additional considerations around caching, query complexity, and security.

For beginners, it's useful to be aware of GraphQL, but focusing on REST first is a more natural learning curve.

3. SOAP (Simple Object Access Protocol)

SOAP is an older API protocol standard that was widely used in enterprise software systems before REST rose to dominance.

Key Characteristics of SOAP APIs:

- **XML-Based:** SOAP uses XML exclusively for messaging, which makes messages heavier and more verbose compared to JSON.

- **Strict Standards:** SOAP APIs follow rigid rules and security standards (WS-Security), making them suitable for enterprise-grade, high-security environments.

- **Formal Contracts:** SOAP APIs define strict contracts (WSDL — Web Services Description Language) describing exactly what operations are available and how to interact with them.

Example:
A SOAP request to fetch a customer record would be a highly structured XML document rather than a simple URL call.

While SOAP is powerful and still critical in industries like finance, insurance, and healthcare, it's relatively heavy and complex compared to REST. Most modern public APIs (especially those intended for mobile and web apps) prefer REST or GraphQL today.

As a beginner, it's important to **understand SOAP exists** and **appreciate why REST and GraphQL became more popular** for newer development.

Quick Comparison:

Feature	REST	GraphQL	SOAP
Data Format	Typically JSON	Specific query language	XML only
Flexibility	Medium	High (select fields)	Low (fixed schema)
Ease of Use	High (simple HTTP requests)	Medium (needs learning query)	Low (complex XML messages)
Use Cases	Web and mobile APIs	Dynamic, flexible apps	Enterprise apps, strict security

1.4 Why Learning API Development is a Game Changer

In the modern digital world, understanding how to build APIs isn't just another technical skill — it's a career-defining advantage and a massive personal unlock. Whether you want to build your own apps, work for a tech giant, freelance, or launch a startup, mastering API development positions you ahead of the curve.

1. APIs Are the Foundation of Modern Apps

Behind every successful modern application — from social media networks to fintech platforms, ride-sharing apps, streaming services, e-commerce giants — APIs act as the central nervous system. Without APIs, none of the seamless user experiences we take for granted would exist.

Learning API development means you understand how applications actually **communicate, exchange data**, and **coordinate services**. You are no longer confined to building isolated apps; you gain the ability to build systems that interact with countless other platforms, scaling your capabilities exponentially.

2. APIs Open Up Endless Opportunities for Integration

When you know how to develop APIs, you are no longer limited to the boundaries of your own code. You can:

- Integrate payment gateways like Stripe or PayPal into your app,

- Connect with cloud services like AWS, Azure, or Google Cloud,

- Plug into communication platforms like Twilio (SMS), Slack (messaging), or Zoom (video calls),

- Pull external data like news, sports scores, or market prices,

- Power connections with IoT devices, smart homes, or wearable tech.

The possibilities are endless — and they all hinge on API skills.

When you can build your own APIs and consume others', you are no longer working in isolation. You are building applications that **live in the real world**, interacting seamlessly with ecosystems that users already trust and depend on.

3. APIs Are the Future of Business

Modern businesses are shifting from monolithic software models to **microservices, serverless architectures**, and **cloud-first strategies**. In each of these models, APIs are the glue that binds independent services together.

Even non-tech industries are realizing the power of APIs:

- Banks are adopting open banking APIs.

- Healthcare providers are using APIs to share medical data securely.

- Governments are rolling out open data APIs.

- Transportation companies are offering APIs for ticketing, tracking, and reservations.

The demand for API developers is growing not only in pure tech companies but across almost every sector. If you can design secure, scalable APIs, you become a valuable player in any industry.

4. API Skills Future-Proof Your Career

Technology stacks change. Programming languages come and go. Frameworks rise and fall in popularity.
But the core principle of **building software systems that communicate reliably and securely** is not going anywhere.

By learning API development:

- You build a skill that stays relevant across evolving tech landscapes.

- You make yourself adaptable to new tools, protocols, and technologies.

- You anchor your career not in fleeting trends, but in foundational knowledge.

When you understand the principles of API development — abstraction, communication protocols, security, data serialization, versioning, documentation — you can apply them whether you are using Flask today, FastAPI tomorrow, or some yet-to-be-invented tool five years from now.

5. APIs Empower Innovation

At a personal level, API skills are profoundly empowering. Once you know how to create and connect services, you can:

- Build your own SaaS (Software as a Service) product,

- Automate business processes,

- Create platforms that interact with other apps,

- Build portfolios that stand out from the crowd,

- Rapidly prototype startup ideas without needing massive teams.

Understanding APIs gives you leverage: **you stop being dependent solely on frontend features** and **start building full systems** that can grow, evolve, and scale.

In short, learning API development is not just another skill on your résumé. It's a transformative capability that unlocks real-world power — to build better products, to collaborate more effectively, and to create opportunities that would otherwise remain closed.

You are not just learning to code; you are learning to **build bridges**, **create platforms**, and **connect worlds**.

1.5 API Development: Essential Skills and Career Advantages

Now that you see why learning API development is such a game changer, it's important to understand exactly **which skills** API development builds — and **how those skills set you apart** in the real-world job market and project landscape.

Let's break it down.

1. Core Technical Skills You Gain

a. HTTP and Web Fundamentals Mastery

API development forces you to deeply understand HTTP — the protocol that powers the entire web. You will master:

- How requests and responses work,

- HTTP methods (GET, POST, PUT, DELETE),

- Status codes (200 OK, 404 Not Found, 500 Internal Server Error),

- Headers, cookies, authentication flows.

This knowledge is transferable to frontend development, backend development, networking, cybersecurity, cloud computing, and more.

b. Backend Development Skills

As you build APIs, you naturally learn how backend systems work:

- Handling server requests,

- Managing databases and data storage,

- Processing logic on the server side,

- Structuring scalable application architectures.

You become comfortable with the server side of development — a crucial skill that makes you much more versatile.

c. Data Formats and Serialization

APIs often exchange data in structured formats, primarily JSON and sometimes XML. You'll learn:

- How to design and parse JSON objects,

- How to serialize (convert into a transmission format) and deserialize (convert back into usable data),

- How to structure responses for efficiency and clarity.

This makes your data-handling skills sharper and prepares you for working with databases, APIs, and data pipelines.

d. Security Fundamentals

Even at a beginner level, API development introduces you to essential security principles:

- Protecting endpoints with authentication,

- Safeguarding user data,

- Preventing common attacks (like SQL injection, CSRF),

- Implementing secure API keys and tokens.

Security is a fundamental pillar of professional software development, and API work grounds you in these best practices early.

e. Documentation and Communication Skills

APIs without documentation are useless. As an API developer, you'll learn how to:

- Write clear API documentation,

- Specify request formats, parameters, expected responses,

- Communicate technical concepts clearly for others to use your APIs.

These skills translate directly into teamwork, open-source contribution, freelance work, and enterprise collaboration.

2. Career Advantages of API Development Skills

a. High Demand Across Industries

Every industry that builds software needs API developers — not just big tech companies.
Finance, healthcare, government, media, education, logistics, and countless other sectors rely on APIs. Your skills are universally in demand.

b. Opportunities in High-Paying Roles

Many lucrative career paths directly involve API work, including:

- Backend Developer

- Full Stack Developer

- Cloud Developer

- Integration Engineer

- API Product Manager

- Solution Architect

- Platform Engineer

These roles often pay higher than purely frontend-focused roles because they involve building critical infrastructure and ensuring secure, scalable system communication.

c. Remote and Freelance Flexibility

API work lends itself beautifully to remote jobs and freelancing. Many startups, agencies, and companies hire remote API developers for:

- Building internal services,

- Integrating third-party APIs,

- Building MVPs (Minimum Viable Products),

- Extending existing platforms.

You can work on meaningful projects from anywhere in the world once you have strong API skills and a portfolio to showcase them.

d. Entrepreneurial Independence

If you ever want to launch your own product, SaaS startup, or side project, API skills are invaluable. You can:

- Build the backend yourself,

- Integrate third-party services,

- Launch faster without needing to outsource core functionality.

Technical independence translates into faster innovation, lower costs, and higher creative freedom.

e. Future-Proofing Your Skillset

As the world continues moving toward microservices, cloud-native architectures, and interconnected ecosystems, API development will only become more essential.

Knowing how to design, build, secure, and maintain APIs ensures that you remain adaptable — ready to work with the next generation of tools, services, and systems that emerge.

Chapter 2: The Basics of Web Communication

2.1 How the Internet and Web Requests Work

Before you can build APIs that communicate effectively, you must first understand **how the Internet itself handles communication**. The Internet is not some magical force connecting computers — it's a vast, structured network built upon layers of standards and protocols.

At its most fundamental level, the Internet operates like a giant postal system. It delivers digital "letters" (data packets) from one machine to another, across cities, countries, and continents. But unlike a postal service that uses paper envelopes, the Internet uses a collection of highly organized technologies.

Let's break this down into the essentials you need to grasp.

What Happens When You Access a Website?

Suppose you type www.example.com into your browser and hit Enter. Behind the scenes, the following steps happen rapidly:

1. **DNS Lookup:**
   Your computer asks the Domain Name System (DNS) servers, "What is the IP address of www.example.com?"
   DNS servers respond with the IP address (something like 93.184.216.34) associated with that domain name.

2. **TCP Connection:**
   Your computer initiates a connection to that IP address using a protocol called TCP (Transmission Control Protocol), ensuring that the two machines agree on how to communicate reliably.

3. **HTTP Request:**
   Your browser sends an HTTP request over that connection, asking, "Please give me the home page (index page) of this website."

4. **Server Response:**
   The server processes the request and sends back an HTTP response, including the content of the web page (HTML, images, stylesheets, etc.).

5. **Browser Rendering:**
   Your browser receives the response and renders the website on your screen.

All of this happens in milliseconds. Each step follows precise protocols to ensure that the communication is clear, efficient, and reliable — even if the servers are halfway across the world.

Clients and Servers

In Internet communication, two primary actors are always involved:

- **Client:**
  The entity making the request (e.g., your web browser, a mobile app, or an API consumer).

- **Server:**
  The entity processing the request and sending back a response (e.g., a web server hosting a website or an API server providing data).

In API development, you are usually **building the server** side — the part that listens for requests, processes them, and sends back meaningful responses.

The Role of Protocols

Protocols are agreed-upon rules that govern how communication happens.
For web-based communication, the most critical protocol is **HTTP** — Hypertext Transfer Protocol.

When you build or consume APIs, you are really participating in an **exchange of HTTP requests and responses** — a structured conversation between clients and servers.

Understanding **how web requests work** and **how HTTP governs them** is crucial before you start designing and building your own APIs.

2.2 HTTP Protocol Essentials

HTTP — Hypertext Transfer Protocol — is the foundation of data communication for the web.

When two machines need to talk over the Internet, HTTP defines **how to format the request**, **how to format the response**, and **what each part of the conversation means**.

Let's break down the essentials of HTTP you need to know for API development.

Structure of an HTTP Request

When a client (like a web browser or a mobile app) wants to request something from a server, it sends an HTTP Request composed of several key parts:

Request Line:
Specifies the HTTP method (such as GET or POST), the URL (or path), and the HTTP version.

Example:

```bash
CopyEdit
GET /api/users HTTP/1.1
```

- **Headers:**
  Metadata about the request. Headers tell the server important things like what type of content is being sent or what kind of response is expected.

  Example:

  ```pgsql
  CopyEdit
  Content-Type: application/json
  ```

  Authorization: Bearer <token>

- **Body:**
  Optional data sent with the request. Not all requests have bodies (e.g., GET usually does not). But POST, PUT, PATCH requests often carry data (like user input or file uploads) inside the body.

24

Example (body content for a POST request):

json
CopyEdit
```
{
  "username": "johndoe",
  "email": "john@example.com"
}
```

Structure of an HTTP Response

When the server processes the request, it sends back an HTTP Response structured as follows:

Status Line:
Indicates whether the request was successful or failed, using a status code and a short description.

Example:

CopyEdit
```
HTTP/1.1 200 OK
```

Headers:
Provide metadata about the response, such as content type, caching policies, or server information.

Example:

pgsql
CopyEdit
```
Content-Type: application/json
```

Body:
Contains the actual data returned by the server (e.g., requested information, confirmation messages, error details).

Example (body content for a successful API response):

```json
CopyEdit
{
  "id": 1,
  "username": "johndoe",
  "email": "john@example.com"
}
```

Important HTTP Status Codes

When building APIs, understanding status codes is vital for providing meaningful feedback to clients.

Status Code	Meaning	Use Case
200	OK	Successful request.
201	Created	Resource successfully created.
400	Bad Request	Malformed request from client.
401	Unauthorized	Authentication required.
403	Forbidden	Access denied.
404	Not Found	Requested resource doesn't exist.
500	Internal Server Error	Server-side problem occurred.

When designing APIs, using the correct status codes makes your services more professional, easier to debug, and easier for other developers to consume.

2.3 HTTP Methods: GET, POST, PUT, PATCH, DELETE

HTTP methods — often called **verbs** — define the type of action the client wants the server to perform. In API development, using the correct method for each operation is a critical part of good design.

Let's explore the five core HTTP methods that you will use when building RESTful APIs.

1. GET

Purpose:
Retrieve data from the server.

Key Characteristics:

- Safe (does not change server state).

- Idempotent (multiple identical requests have the same effect).

- Data sent through query parameters, not the body.

Example Request:

```
http
CopyEdit
GET /api/users/1
```

Example Usage:

- Fetch user details.

- Get a list of blog posts.

- Retrieve product inventory.

2. POST

Purpose:
Send data to the server to create a new resource.

Key Characteristics:

- Changes server state (creates something new).

- Not idempotent (sending the same request multiple times creates multiple resources).

Example Request:

http
CopyEdit
POST /api/users
Content-Type: application/json

```
{
 "username": "newuser",
 "email": "newuser@example.com"
}
```

Example Usage:

- Create a new user account.

- Submit a new order.

- Add a comment to a blog post.

3. PUT

Purpose:
Update an existing resource completely.

Key Characteristics:

- Idempotent (sending the same request multiple times results in the same state).

- Requires the full resource representation to be sent in the request.

Example Request:

http
CopyEdit
PUT /api/users/1
Content-Type: application/json

{
  "username": "updateduser",
  "email": "updated@example.com"
}

Example Usage:

- Update all fields of a user profile.

- Replace an article's content.

4. PATCH

Purpose:
Update part of an existing resource.

Key Characteristics:

- Partially updates a resource (only specified fields).

- More efficient than PUT when updating a few fields.

- Also idempotent when designed properly.

Example Request:

http
CopyEdit
PATCH /api/users/1
Content-Type: application/json

29

```
{
  "email": "newemail@example.com"
}
```

Example Usage:

- Update just the email of a user without affecting other fields.

- Change the status of an order.

5. DELETE

Purpose:
Remove a resource from the server.

Key Characteristics:

- Idempotent (repeated delete requests on the same resource have the same effect: the resource is gone).

- May return 204 (No Content) or 200 with a confirmation.

Example Request:

```
http
CopyEdit
DELETE /api/users/1
```

Example Usage:

- Delete a user account.

- Remove a product from inventory.

- Cancel a subscription.

Summary Table of HTTP Methods:

Method	Action	Idempotent	Typical Usage
GET	Retrieve resource(s)	Yes	Fetch data
POST	Create new resource	No	Add new data
PUT	Update/replace entire resource	Yes	Full update of a record
PATCH	Update part of a resource	Yes	Partial update (specific fields)
DELETE	Remove a resource	Yes	Delete a record

2.4 Status Codes: 200s, 400s, 500s Explained

When two machines communicate over the Internet — whether a browser talking to a web server, or a mobile app talking to an API — they need a clear way to indicate whether a request succeeded or failed, and why. This is where **HTTP status codes** come into play.

Status codes are **three-digit numbers** returned in every HTTP response. They tell the client (you, or the application making the request) what happened — without needing to parse the entire response body.

Understanding and properly using status codes is a **critical part of building professional APIs**. Let's break down the most important groups you need to know.

1. 200s: Success Codes

These codes indicate that the request was successfully received, understood, and processed by the server.

Key 200-series status codes:

- **200 OK:**
  The request succeeded. This is the most common status for a successful GET or PUT request.

  Example: Retrieving a user's profile.

- **201 Created:**
  The request succeeded, and a new resource was created.
  Common after successful POST requests (like creating a new account).

31

Example: User registration.

- **202 Accepted:**
  The request has been accepted for processing, but the processing is not yet complete.
  Often used for asynchronous operations.

  Example: Submitting a long-running report generation job.

- **204 No Content:**
  The request succeeded, but there is no content to return.
  Often used after DELETE operations.

  Example: Deleting a user account.

2. 400s: Client Error Codes

These codes indicate that the problem came from the **client's side** — meaning the request was somehow incorrect, malformed, or unauthorized.

Key 400-series status codes:

- **400 Bad Request:**
  The server cannot or will not process the request due to something that is perceived to be a client error.

  Example: Sending invalid JSON in a request body.

- **401 Unauthorized:**
  The client must authenticate itself to get the requested response.

  Example: Trying to access user data without a valid API token.

- **403 Forbidden:**
  The client is authenticated, but does not have permission to access the resource.

  Example: Trying to delete another user's account.

- **404 Not Found:**
  The server cannot find the requested resource.

  Example: Requesting a non-existent product or page.

- **409 Conflict:**
  The request could not be completed because of a conflict with the current state of the resource.

  Example: Trying to create a duplicate user account where the username must be unique.

- **422 Unprocessable Entity:**
  The server understands the content type of the request but was unable to process the contained instructions.

  Example: Failing form validation when creating or updating a record.

3. 500s: Server Error Codes

These codes indicate that the server **encountered an error** and could not fulfill a seemingly valid request.

Key 500-series status codes:

- **500 Internal Server Error:**
  The server encountered an unexpected condition that prevented it from fulfilling the request.

  Example: Bug or crash inside the server code.

- **502 Bad Gateway:**
  The server, while acting as a gateway or proxy, received an invalid response from an upstream server.

  Example: Your API depends on another external API that is down.

- **503 Service Unavailable:**
  The server is currently unable to handle the request due to maintenance or

overload.

Example: Server is undergoing maintenance or experiencing traffic spikes.

- **504 Gateway Timeout:**
  The server, while acting as a gateway or proxy, did not receive a timely response from an upstream server.

  Example: Third-party service your API relies on is too slow to respond.

Why Proper Status Codes Matter

- They help clients programmatically understand what went wrong.

- They make debugging much easier.

- They improve the overall developer experience when other developers consume your APIs.

- They help maintain standards and professionalism in your API design.

As an API developer, **sending the right status codes** is as important as **sending the right data**. Always think carefully about how to respond to success, errors, and unexpected situations.

2.5 Anatomy of a Web API Request and Response

Now that you have a solid understanding of status codes, it's time to look more closely at the **full structure** of an API conversation: the **Request** and the **Response**.

When building APIs, you'll constantly design both sides of this exchange. Let's go step-by-step.

The API Request Structure

When a client sends a request to your API, it typically includes:

1. **HTTP Method:**
   Specifies what action the client wants to perform (GET, POST, PUT, PATCH, DELETE).

2. **URL/Endpoint:**
   The specific resource or service being requested.

Example:

arduino
CopyEdit
https://api.example.com/users/123

3. **Headers:**
   Metadata about the request. Important headers include:

   o Content-Type: What format the request body is in (e.g., application/json).

   o Authorization: Credentials like an API key or token.

   o Accept: What response format the client expects (usually application/json).

Query Parameters (Optional):
Key-value pairs added to the URL to filter or modify the request.

Example:

bash
CopyEdit
GET /products?category=books&price_lt=50

Body (Optional):
Data sent with the request, usually in POST, PUT, or PATCH operations.

Example (POST body):

json
CopyEdit

```
{
  "username": "newuser",
  "email": "newuser@example.com"
}
```

Not every request needs every component. For instance, a simple GET request might not need a body at all.

The API Response Structure

When your server processes the request, it sends a response back to the client with the following components:

1. **Status Code:**
   Indicates whether the request was successful or what kind of error occurred.

2. **Headers:**
   Metadata about the response.

   o Content-Type: Usually application/json.

   o Cache-Control: Instructions about caching the response.

   o Authorization-Info: May carry new tokens in certain flows.

Body:
The main data returned.
Even in error cases, it's good practice to include a structured error message.

Example (Successful response):

json
CopyEdit
```
{
  "id": 123,
  "username": "newuser",
  "email": "newuser@example.com"
}
```

Example (Error response):

json
CopyEdit
```
{
  "error": "User not found",
  "status": 404
}
```

Tip:
Good APIs make sure that even error messages follow a consistent and predictable format.
This helps client developers handle errors gracefully without confusion.

A Simple Example: Full Request-Response

Suppose a client wants to create a new user account.

Client Request:

http
CopyEdit
```
POST /api/users HTTP/1.1
Host: api.example.com
Content-Type: application/json
Authorization: Bearer abcdef123456

{
  "username": "johndoe",
```

37

```
"email": "john@example.com",
"password": "supersecret"
}
```

Server Response:

http
CopyEdit
HTTP/1.1 201 Created
Content-Type: application/json

```
{
  "id": 789,
  "username": "johndoe",
  "email": "john@example.com",
  "created_at": "2025-04-25T14:32:00Z"
}
```

Both sides are clearly structured:

- The **Request** indicates what the client wants.

- The **Response** indicates what happened and what data the server is sending back.

This simple, structured communication is the heart of API development.

Mastering the anatomy of requests and responses early will save you countless hours of debugging, testing, and client support work in the future.

Chapter 3: Introduction to REST API Principles

3.1 What Makes an API RESTful?

When people talk about building modern APIs, especially for web and mobile applications, they almost always mention **REST**.
 But what exactly does it mean for an API to be **RESTful**?

To understand this, let's start with the basics.

REST stands for **Representational State Transfer**. It's an architectural style proposed by computer scientist Roy Fielding in his PhD dissertation in 2000. REST is not a protocol or a strict set of rules; it is a set of **design principles** intended to create scalable, reliable, and easy-to-use web services.

When we say an API is **RESTful**, we mean that it follows the key principles of REST.

Here are the major characteristics that define a RESTful API:

1. Statelessness

In REST, every API request from a client must contain all the information the server needs to fulfill that request.
 The server does not remember anything about the client's previous interactions.

Each request is treated independently.

This makes REST APIs:

- Scalable (because servers don't have to keep track of client sessions),

- Easier to maintain (less server memory used),

- More reliable (crashes or failures affect fewer clients).

2. Uniform Interface

All interactions between the client and server happen through a **standardized interface**.

In REST APIs, this typically means:

- Using consistent HTTP methods (GET, POST, PUT, DELETE),

- Using meaningful URLs to access resources,

- Using standard HTTP status codes to indicate outcomes,

- Delivering resources in standard formats like JSON.

By following a uniform interface, REST APIs become predictable, intuitive, and easier for developers to use.

3. Resource-Based

A RESTful API treats everything as a **resource**.
A resource could be:

- A user,

- A blog post,

- An order,

- A comment,

- A product.

Each resource is identified by a **URL (Uniform Resource Locator)**.

Example:

arduino
CopyEdit
https://api.example.com/users/123

Here, /users/123 points to the user resource with ID 123.

4. Client-Server Separation

REST enforces a **clear separation of concerns** between the client and the server.

- The **client** is responsible for the user interface and user experience.

- The **server** is responsible for processing requests, managing resources, and responding.

This separation allows teams to work independently on frontend and backend, and it enables each side to evolve separately.

5. Representation of Resources

Clients interact with resources through **representations**, often in JSON format.

For example, when a client asks for a user resource, the server might respond with a JSON object representing that user:

json
CopyEdit

```
{
  "id": 123,
  "name": "John Doe",
  "email": "john@example.com"
}
```

The client doesn't need to know how the server stores or manages that user internally — it only cares about the representation it receives.

6. Stateless Communication over HTTP

REST APIs generally use HTTP as the communication protocol.

All actions (reading, writing, updating, deleting) are performed via standard HTTP methods (verbs).
This keeps REST APIs simple and consistent with web standards.

In Summary:

An API is **RESTful** if it:

- Treats data and functionality as resources,

- Uses HTTP methods to operate on these resources,

- Follows stateless communication,

- Presents a uniform, predictable interface,

- Transfers representations (usually JSON),

- Separates client and server responsibilities.

Understanding these fundamentals is essential because **REST shapes how you design APIs**, **how you name endpoints**, **how you handle data**, and **how you structure your overall service.**

3.2 Resources, Endpoints, and Methods

In REST API design, the **three pillars** you must master early are **Resources, Endpoints**, and **Methods**.
These concepts define how clients interact with your service — and getting them right makes your APIs easy to understand, use, and maintain.

Let's dive into each one.

1. Resources

A **resource** is anything that can be named and accessed via an API.

It could be:

- A **user**,
- A **product**,
- A **comment**,
- A **photo**,
- A **payment transaction**.

Each resource is an object with attributes.
For example, a **User** resource might have:

- id
- name
- email
- created_at
- updated_at

In REST, resources are the **center of the universe**.
Everything you do revolves around **managing resources** — creating them, reading them, updating them, and deleting them.

2. Endpoints

An **endpoint** is a **URL that represents a resource** or a **collection of resources**.

Endpoints are how clients specify **which resource** they want to interact with.

Good RESTful endpoints follow a clear, consistent pattern.

Examples:

- GET /users → Retrieve all users.

- GET /users/123 → Retrieve a specific user with ID 123.

- POST /users → Create a new user.

- PUT /users/123 → Update user with ID 123.

- DELETE /users/123 → Delete user with ID 123.

Notice a few things:

- **Plural nouns** are usually used (/users, not /user).

- **Resource IDs** are placed in the URL path (/users/123).

- The URL describes the **resource**, and the **HTTP method** describes the **action**.

This keeps the API intuitive.
 A developer can often guess what an endpoint does just by looking at the URL and method.

3. Methods

We already touched on HTTP methods in the previous chapter, but let's now tie them specifically to resource actions:

HTTP Method	Action	Example Endpoint	Purpose
GET	Read (Retrieve)	GET /users or GET /users/123	Fetch one or many resources
POST	Create	POST /users	Create a new resource
PUT	Update (Replace)	PUT /users/123	Replace an existing resource completely
PATCH	Update (Partial)	PATCH /users/123	Modify an existing resource (partially)
DELETE	Delete	DELETE /users/123	Remove a resource

By **combining resources, endpoints, and methods**, you design the public face of your API — the way others will interact with your service.

Good design principles ensure that:

- APIs are predictable,

- Errors are minimized,

- Developers love using your API instead of struggling with it.

3.3 Understanding CRUD Operations

When building REST APIs, almost everything revolves around performing **CRUD operations** on resources.

CRUD stands for:

- **Create**

- **Read**

- **Update**

- **Delete**

These operations mirror real-world interactions with data and are directly tied to HTTP methods.

Let's explore each one carefully.

1. Create (POST)

Purpose:
Add a new resource.

How:
Send a POST request to the collection endpoint.

Example:

http
CopyEdit
POST /users
Content-Type: application/json

```
{
  "name": "Alice Smith",
  "email": "alice@example.com"
}
```

Server Response:

- 201 Created

- Body with the new user's details, including a unique ID.

2. Read (GET)

Purpose:
Retrieve existing resources.

How:
Use a GET request.

Examples:

Fetch all users:

bash
CopyEdit
GET /users

Fetch a single user by ID:

```bash
CopyEdit
GET /users/123
```

Server Response:

- 200 OK

- JSON array (for multiple resources) or JSON object (for a single resource).

3. Update (PUT or PATCH)

Purpose:
Modify an existing resource.

How:

- PUT to **replace** the entire resource.

- PATCH to **modify** specific fields only.

Examples:

Replace entire user record:

```http
CopyEdit
PUT /users/123
Content-Type: application/json

{
  "name": "Alice B. Smith",
  "email": "aliceb@example.com"
}
```

47

Update just the email:

```http
CopyEdit
PATCH /users/123
Content-Type: application/json

{
  "email": "newalice@example.com"
}
```

Server Response:

- 200 OK or 204 No Content.

4. Delete (DELETE)

Purpose:
Remove an existing resource.

How:
Send a DELETE request.

Example:

```http
CopyEdit
DELETE /users/123
```

Server Response:

- 204 No Content (no body, just confirmation the resource was deleted).

CRUD Operations Summary:

Operation	HTTP Method	Typical Endpoint	Response Code
Create	POST	/users	201 Created
Read	GET	/users or /users/123	200 OK
Update	PUT or PATCH	/users/123	200 OK or 204 No Content
Delete	DELETE	/users/123	204 No Content

3.4 Statelessness, Cacheability, and Layered Systems

When designing RESTful APIs, it's not just about creating endpoints and handling CRUD operations.
 REST as an architectural style has deeper principles that make services **scalable**, **robust**, and **high-performing** — especially important as your applications grow.

Three key principles to understand are **Statelessness**, **Cacheability**, and **Layered Systems**.

Let's dive into each one carefully.

Statelessness

Definition:
 In REST, **each request from a client to the server must contain all the information needed to understand and process the request**. The server must **not store any information about the client** between requests.

In simple terms:

> Every request is self-contained.
> The server treats each request like a clean slate.

Why is Statelessness Important?

- **Scalability:**
   Because the server does not need to remember anything about previous requests,

it can easily scale to serve millions of independent clients without tracking sessions.

- **Reliability:**
  If a server crashes or needs to be replaced, there's no lost session data. Clients simply send their next request as normal.

- **Simplicity:**
  Stateless servers are easier to maintain and troubleshoot.

Example of Statelessness in APIs:

Imagine a client requesting user profile information.
Instead of assuming the server knows who the user is based on a previous login, the client must **include credentials** (like an API key or token) **with every request**.

```http
http
CopyEdit
GET /profile
Authorization: Bearer abc123xyz
```

The server reads the token, verifies it, fetches the appropriate data, and sends the response.
It does not remember who you are after the response — it forgets everything.

Cacheability

Definition:
In REST, responses from the server should **explicitly indicate whether they are cacheable or not**.
If a response is cacheable, it can be stored by the client or by intermediaries (like proxies), reducing the need to fetch the same data repeatedly.

Why Cacheability Matters:

- **Performance Boost:**
  Cached data loads faster for users because it doesn't need to be fetched from the server again.

- **Reduced Server Load:**
  Servers handle fewer requests, saving resources and bandwidth.

- **Better Scalability:**
  Caching helps your APIs handle more users without scaling up infrastructure aggressively.

How APIs Indicate Cacheability:

Through HTTP Headers like:

- Cache-Control: public, max-age=3600 (cache for 1 hour),

- ETag (entity tag used for validating cached responses).

Example:

http
CopyEdit
GET /products/42
Cache-Control: max-age=3600

This tells the client it's safe to cache this product's data for 3600 seconds (one hour).

Layered Systems

Definition:
A RESTful system can be composed of **multiple layers**, and clients should not be able to tell whether they are connected directly to the end server or to an intermediary (like a load balancer, proxy, or cache server).

Each layer **only knows about the layer it communicates with directly**.

Why Layered Systems Matter:

- **Scalability:**
  You can add load balancers, caches, gateways, or security filters without

changing client behavior.

- **Security:**
  Middle layers can enforce authentication, encryption, or rate limiting.

- **Maintainability:**
  Systems can be updated or scaled independently at different layers without affecting the whole architecture.

Real-World Example:

When a mobile app connects to an API, the connection might first hit:

- A **CDN** (Content Delivery Network),

- Then a **load balancer**,

- Then an **API Gateway**,

- And finally the **actual application server**.

The mobile app has no idea about these layers — and it doesn't need to.

This abstraction is what makes RESTful systems **resilient**, **scalable**, and **secure** at scale.

3.5 REST API Design Best Practices

Now that you understand the deeper REST principles, let's talk about **practical design best practices** you should always follow when building APIs.

Professional API developers aren't just judged by whether their code "works" — they are judged by how intuitive, consistent, and maintainable their APIs are.

Following best practices makes other developers love using your APIs — and trust your work.

1. Use Nouns, Not Verbs, in Endpoints

In REST, **URLs represent resources** — so **nouns** should be used in endpoint names, not verbs.

Good:

```bash
CopyEdit
GET /users
POST /products
DELETE /orders/123
```

Avoid:

```bash
CopyEdit
GET /getUsers
POST /createProduct
DELETE /deleteOrder/123
```

The HTTP method already describes the action (GET, POST, DELETE), so the endpoint itself should simply describe **what** you are acting upon.

2. Keep URLs Simple and Predictable

Make your API URLs:

- **Consistent** (/users/123/orders/456 not /users/123/order/456info),

- **Lowercase** (avoid uppercase letters),

- **Hyphenated** if needed (not camelCase).

Good URLs are easy to read and guess without constant documentation checks.

3. Use HTTP Status Codes Properly

Always respond with the appropriate HTTP status code.

- **200 OK** for successful GETs,

- **201 Created** after a successful POST,

- **204 No Content** after DELETEs,

- **400 Bad Request** for validation errors,

- **401 Unauthorized** when authentication fails,

- **404 Not Found** when the resource doesn't exist,

- **500 Internal Server Error** when something goes wrong on the server.

Don't always return 200 for everything — be intentional.

4. Support Filtering, Sorting, and Pagination

For collection endpoints (like getting a list of users, products, or articles), allow clients to:

- **Filter** results (e.g., by date, status, category),

- **Sort** results (e.g., newest first, alphabetical order),

- **Paginate** results (e.g., 10 users per page).

Example of good filtering and pagination:

bash
CopyEdit
GET /products?category=books&sort=price_desc&page=2&page_size=10

This makes your API more powerful and scalable.

54

5. Design Error Responses Clearly

When something goes wrong, send helpful, structured error messages.

Example of a good error response:

```json
CopyEdit
{
  "error": "Validation Failed",
  "details": {
    "email": "Email must be a valid format",
    "password": "Password must be at least 8 characters"
  },
  "status": 400
}
```

This is much better than returning vague messages like "Something went wrong."

Clear errors help clients understand and fix problems faster.

6. Version Your API

APIs evolve over time. Changes are inevitable.
To avoid breaking existing clients, version your API from day one.

Common ways to version:

- In the URL: /api/v1/users

- In a custom header: Accept: application/vnd.example.v1+json

Versioning allows you to introduce new features or improvements without disrupting older clients.

7. Secure Sensitive Endpoints

Protect your APIs:

- Require **Authentication** (API keys, OAuth tokens, JWTs),

- Enforce **Authorization** (only allow access to permitted users),

- Use **HTTPS** always to encrypt data,

- Validate and sanitize all input to prevent injection attacks.

Security is not optional — especially for APIs that handle personal, financial, or private data.

8. Document Your API

Even the most beautifully designed API is useless if developers don't know how to use it.

Great API documentation includes:

- Clear endpoint lists,

- Expected request formats,

- Sample responses,

- Authentication instructions,

- Error code explanations.

Tools like Swagger (OpenAPI) can help generate interactive, easy-to-read documentation.

Chapter 4: Understanding Data Formats — JSON, XML, and Beyond

4.1 Why JSON Dominates API Communication

When APIs communicate, they need a way to represent and transfer data in a format that both the client and server understand.
 While there are several formats available — XML, YAML, Protocol Buffers, and others — **JSON** has emerged as the undisputed champion for most modern web and mobile APIs.

But why has JSON become the dominant format?
 To understand its popularity, let's look at its key advantages.

1. Simplicity and Readability

JSON (JavaScript Object Notation) was designed to be **lightweight, easy to read**, and **easy to write**.

A JSON object is visually intuitive:

```json
CopyEdit
{
  "id": 123,
  "name": "Alice",
  "email": "alice@example.com"
}
```

- It uses a straightforward structure of **key-value pairs**.

- There's no unnecessary overhead — no verbose opening and closing tags like in XML.

- Both humans and machines can read and understand JSON easily, making debugging and development much faster.

This simplicity is a massive advantage during both development and maintenance.

2. Native Compatibility with JavaScript

Because JSON's syntax is based on JavaScript objects, it is **natively supported** by web browsers and JavaScript environments without needing extra parsing tools.

In JavaScript, converting JSON data into usable objects takes just a single line:

```javascript
CopyEdit
const user = JSON.parse(jsonString);
```

Sending data back to the server is just as easy:

```javascript
CopyEdit
const jsonString = JSON.stringify(user);
```

Given the explosion of JavaScript on both the frontend (React, Angular, Vue) and backend (Node.js), JSON's seamless integration became a natural standard.

3. Lightweight and Efficient

Compared to formats like XML, JSON:

- Requires **fewer characters** to represent the same data,

- Is **smaller in file size**, which means faster transmission over networks,

- Is **quicker to parse** because of its simpler structure.

Smaller payloads and faster parsing times directly translate to **better performance** — crucial in a world where users expect instant responses, especially on mobile networks.

4. Language-Agnostic

Even though JSON is based on JavaScript, it is **supported across virtually all modern programming languages** — Python, Java, C#, Go, Ruby, PHP, Swift, and many more.

Almost every language provides libraries or built-in functionality to parse and generate JSON easily.
 This makes JSON a perfect "common language" for APIs, no matter which tech stack is involved.

5. Structured Yet Flexible

JSON supports nested structures — meaning you can represent complex data with relative ease:

json
CopyEdit
```
{
  "user": {
    "id": 1,
    "name": "Alice",
    "contacts": [
      {"type": "email", "value": "alice@example.com"},
      {"type": "phone", "value": "123-456-7890"}
    ]
  }
}
```

You can model relationships, hierarchies, arrays, and optional fields without much friction.
 This flexibility makes JSON ideal for a wide range of APIs — from simple CRUD applications to sophisticated microservices.

6. Standardized and Evolving

JSON has formal standards:

- **RFC 8259** defines the JSON specification.

- JSON Schema standards allow APIs to **describe**, **validate**, and **document** JSON data structures formally.

There's also an active community continuously refining how JSON is used in API design.

Real-World Examples

Nearly every major API today uses JSON as its default format:

- Twitter API,

- GitHub API,

- Spotify API,

- Stripe API,

- Google Cloud APIs.

Even when other formats are technically supported (like XML or YAML), **JSON remains the default recommendation** because of its ubiquity and simplicity.

In Summary

JSON dominates API communication because it is:

- Simple,

- Lightweight,

- Human-readable,

- Fast to parse,

- Compatible across platforms,

- Structured yet flexible.

As an API developer, mastering JSON isn't optional — it's essential.
Fortunately, it's also one of the easiest formats to work with.

In the next section, we'll get hands-on with **working with JSON objects and arrays** — the building blocks of API communication.

4.2 Working with JSON Objects and Arrays

Once you understand why JSON is so widely used, the next step is getting comfortable **creating**, **reading**, and **manipulating** JSON data.

At the heart of JSON are two fundamental structures:

- **Objects** (dictionaries of key-value pairs),

- **Arrays** (ordered lists of values).

Let's look at both in detail.

JSON Objects

Definition:
A JSON Object is a collection of **key-value pairs** where:

- Keys are always **strings**,

- Values can be strings, numbers, booleans, arrays, other objects, or null.

Syntax:

- Keys and values are separated by colons (:),

- Pairs are separated by commas (,),

- Entire object is wrapped in { } (curly braces).

Example:

json
CopyEdit

```
{
  "id": 42,
  "name": "Alice Smith",
  "email": "alice@example.com",
  "is_active": true
}
```

- "id", "name", "email", and "is_active" are keys.

- 42, "Alice Smith", "alice@example.com", and true are their respective values.

Real API Example: When you call an API endpoint like /users/42, you might receive:

json
CopyEdit

```
{
  "id": 42,
  "username": "alice42",
  "email": "alice42@example.com",
  "roles": ["user", "admin"]
}
```

Here:

- id is a number,

- username and email are strings,

- roles is an array (more on that soon).

JSON Arrays

Definition:
A JSON Array is an **ordered list** of values.
The values can be:

- Strings,

- Numbers,

- Objects,

- Other arrays,

- Booleans,

- Null.

Syntax:

- Values are separated by commas (,),

- Entire array is wrapped in [] (square brackets).

Example:

json
CopyEdit

```
[
  "apple",
  "banana",
  "cherry"
]
```

This is a simple array of strings.

Arrays of Objects:

Often, in real APIs, arrays contain multiple objects.

Example of a list of users:

json
CopyEdit

```
[
  {
    "id": 1,
    "name": "Alice"
  },
  {
    "id": 2,
    "name": "Bob"
  },
  {
    "id": 3,
    "name": "Charlie"
  }
]
```

Each element of the array is a **full object** representing a user.

64

Real API Example: Calling an API like /users might return:

```json
[
  {
    "id": 10,
    "username": "john_doe"
  },
  {
    "id": 11,
    "username": "jane_doe"
  }
]
```

Clients (like your frontend app) can then loop through the array to display a list of users.

Nesting Objects and Arrays

One of JSON's superpowers is **nesting** — placing objects inside arrays, arrays inside objects, and even deeper combinations.

Example of a nested structure:

```json
{
  "user": {
    "id": 123,
    "name": "Alice",
    "orders": [
      {
        "order_id": 1,
        "total": 19.99
      },
      {
        "order_id": 2,
        "total": 49.50
      }
```

```
        ]
      }
   }
```

Here:

- The user is an object,

- Inside user, orders is an array,

- Each order is itself an object.

Nesting allows you to represent complex relationships naturally and flexibly.

JSON Rules You Must Follow

1. **Keys must be strings, enclosed in double quotes.**
   ■ "name": "Alice"
   ✗ name: "Alice"

2. **Values must be valid types.**
   Allowed types: String, Number, Boolean, Array, Object, Null.

3. **No trailing commas.**
   JSON does **not** allow a comma after the last item in an object or array.

4. **Strict syntax.**
   JSON parsers are unforgiving.
   A single missing quote or extra comma will cause parsing to fail.

Common Mistakes

Forgetting Quotes Around Keys:
Wrong:

```json
CopyEdit
{ name: "Alice" }
```
Correct:

```json
CopyEdit
{ "name": "Alice" }
```

Using Single Quotes:
JSON requires **double quotes** for strings and keys.

Wrong:

```json
CopyEdit
{ 'name': 'Alice' }
```
Correct:

```json
CopyEdit
{ "name": "Alice" }
```

Trailing Commas:
Wrong:

```json
CopyEdit
{
  "name": "Alice",
}
```

67

Correct:

json
CopyEdit
```
{
  "name": "Alice"

     }
```

4.3 Brief Overview: XML, YAML, and When They Matter

While **JSON** dominates modern API communication, it's important to understand that **JSON is not the only data format** out there. Depending on the industry, application, or legacy systems, you might also encounter **XML** and **YAML**.

Each format has its strengths and specific use cases where it shines.
Let's take a practical look at both.

XML (eXtensible Markup Language)

Definition:
XML is a markup language designed to **store and transport data**.
It is both **human-readable** and **machine-readable**, but compared to JSON, it is **more verbose** and **more rigid**.

Example: A Simple XML Document

xml
CopyEdit
```
<user>
  <id>123</id>
  <name>Alice</name>
  <email>alice@example.com</email>
</user>
```

- Data is organized using **tags**.

- Every opening tag (`<name>`) must have a closing tag (`</name>`).

- XML supports attributes, nesting, and strict schemas.

Strengths of XML:

- **Strong Typing and Validation:**
  XML can be validated against schemas (XSD files) to enforce strict data structures.

- **Rich Metadata Support:**
  Through attributes, you can embed extra information easily.

- **Widely Used in Legacy Systems:**
  Older enterprise systems (banking, healthcare, government) often rely heavily on XML.

- **Extensive Tooling:**
  Mature libraries exist for parsing, validating, and transforming XML across all programming languages.

When XML Matters:

- When strict schema enforcement is critical.

- In industries where legacy systems dominate (finance, insurance, healthcare).

- When interacting with SOAP APIs (which use XML exclusively).

YAML (YAML Ain't Markup Language)

Definition:
YAML is a **human-friendly data serialization language** designed for **configuration files** and **data exchange**.

Compared to JSON or XML, YAML is much **cleaner and more readable**, especially for complex nested structures.

Example: A Simple YAML Document

yaml
CopyEdit

```
user:
  id: 123
  name: Alice
  email: alice@example.com
```

- No curly braces { } or quotation marks "" required.

- Indentation (spacing) defines structure — not symbols.

Strengths of YAML:

- **Human-Readable:**
  Clean, minimal syntax.

- **Supports Comments:**
  You can annotate files easily with # comments.

- **Ideal for Configuration:**
  Popular for app settings, CI/CD pipelines, container orchestration (e.g., Docker Compose, Kubernetes manifests).

When YAML Matters:

- When writing **configuration files** (e.g., Docker, Kubernetes, GitHub Actions).

- When you want **high human readability** for complex settings.

- In DevOps and cloud-native environments.

Quick Comparison Table

Feature	JSON	XML	YAML
Human-Readable	High	Medium	Very High
Data Size	Small	Large (more verbose)	Small
Parsing Speed	Fast	Medium	Medium
Common Usage	APIs	Enterprise Systems	Configurations
Comment Support	No	No (but metadata possible)	Yes
Schema Support	Moderate (with JSON Schema)	Strong (XSD)	Moderate

Practical Advice for API Developers

- **Default to JSON** unless your client or industry requires otherwise.

- **Know how to work with XML** if you plan to interact with large corporations, government systems, or healthcare tech.

- **Learn basic YAML** if you plan to work in cloud infrastructure, DevOps, or backend settings involving deployments.

Being flexible with formats makes you a more versatile and professional developer.

4.4 Handling Data Serialization and Parsing

Now that you know about different data formats, it's time to understand two critical operations you'll perform constantly when working with APIs:
 Serialization and **Parsing**.

Let's break these concepts down clearly.

What is Serialization?

Serialization means **converting data from a native format (like a Python object, Java object, etc.) into a format suitable for transmission** — usually JSON, XML, or YAML.

In other words:

> **Serialization turns your in-memory data into a format that can travel across the network.**

Real-Life Example:

You have a user object in Python:

```python
python
CopyEdit
user = {
  "id": 123,
  "name": "Alice",
  "email": "alice@example.com"
}
```

Before sending it in an API response, you serialize it into JSON:

```json
json
CopyEdit
{
  "id": 123,
  "name": "Alice",
  "email": "alice@example.com"
}
```

Now it's ready to be transmitted to a frontend app, another server, or a mobile client.

In Code (Python Example):

```python
python
CopyEdit
import json

user = {
    "id": 123,
    "name": "Alice",
    "email": "alice@example.com"
}

json_string = json.dumps(user)
print(json_string)
```

Output:

```json
json
CopyEdit
{"id": 123, "name": "Alice", "email": "alice@example.com"}
```

What is Parsing?

Parsing is the **reverse of serialization**:
 It means **taking incoming data (JSON, XML, YAML) and converting it into a native programming language structure** that you can work with.

In other words:

> **Parsing turns network data into usable objects inside your program.**

Real-Life Example:

You receive a JSON response from an API:

json
CopyEdit
```
{
  "id": 456,
  "name": "Bob",
  "email": "bob@example.com"
}
```

You parse it into a Python dictionary:

python
CopyEdit
```
import json

json_string = '{"id": 456, "name": "Bob", "email": "bob@example.com"}'
user = json.loads(json_string)

print(user["name"])  # Output: Bob
```

Why Serialization and Parsing Matter in API Development

Serialization and parsing are the **input and output pipelines** for every API interaction.

- When your API sends a response → **Serialize** your data.

- When your API receives a request → **Parse** incoming data.

If either process is handled incorrectly:

- Data could be lost or corrupted,

- Your app might crash on bad input,

- Clients might receive unreadable or broken responses.

Thus, careful, consistent serialization and parsing are **foundational skills** for any API developer.

Common Pitfalls to Avoid

- **Inconsistent Field Names:**
  Ensure that field names match expectations exactly.
  For example, if the frontend expects "userName" but you send "username", things will break.

- **Wrong Data Types:**
  JSON does not differentiate between integers and floats very strictly, but your backend or database might.
  Always validate parsed data carefully.

- **Security Risks:**
  Malicious clients might send huge payloads or invalid data.
  Always **validate** and **sanitize** parsed data before processing it.

- **Encoding Issues:**
  Always use proper character encoding (UTF-8 is standard) when serializing or parsing data.

Bonus Tip: Automated Serialization and Parsing

Modern web frameworks (like Flask, Django, Express, FastAPI) often **handle serialization and parsing for you** — if you structure your data correctly.

For example, using FastAPI in Python:

```python
CopyEdit
from fastapi import FastAPI
from pydantic import BaseModel

app = FastAPI()
```

```
class User(BaseModel):
    id: int
    name: str
    email: str

@app.post("/users")
def create_user(user: User):
    return user
```

Here, FastAPI automatically:

- Parses incoming JSON into a User object,

- Serializes the User object back to JSON for the response.

Learning how frameworks assist with this will make you far more productive.

Chapter 5: Designing Great APIs That Developers Love

5.1 The Art of Resource Naming

When it comes to designing APIs that developers actually enjoy using, **naming matters more than you might think**.
 Clear, consistent resource naming makes an API:

- Easier to understand,

- Easier to guess,

- Easier to maintain,

- And far less frustrating for future developers.

Poor naming, on the other hand, leads to confusion, mistakes, and wasted time.

Great APIs are not just functional — they are **intuitive**, and that intuition starts with naming.

General Principles for Naming Resources

1. **Use Plural Nouns for Collections**

When referring to a set of resources, always use plural nouns.

■ Good:

bash
CopyEdit
```
/users
/products
/orders
```

✖ Bad:

bash
CopyEdit
/user
/product
/order

Plural names make it obvious that the endpoint represents a collection.
When you request /users, it's clear you expect **multiple** users.

2. **Use Singular Nouns for Specific Resources**

When referring to a **specific** resource, use the singular noun along with an **identifier** (usually the resource's ID).

 Good:

bash
CopyEdit
/users/123
/products/456
/orders/789

This pattern creates consistency:

- /users → List all users.

- /users/123 → Get details for user with ID 123.

3. **Be Consistent**

Inconsistency in naming leads to confusion and bugs.
Pick a naming convention early and stick with it across all endpoints.

78

Avoid mixing patterns like:

bash
CopyEdit
```
/users/123
/userprofile/1234
/user_orders/12345
```

Instead, maintain a logical, consistent structure:

bash
CopyEdit
```
/users/123
/users/123/orders
/users/123/profile
```

4. **Use Hyphens to Separate Words**

If your resource name contains multiple words, use **hyphens** (-) to separate them, not underscores (_) or camelCase.

■ Good:

bash
CopyEdit
```
/user-profiles
/order-history
```

✖ Bad:

bash
CopyEdit
```
/user_profiles
/UserProfiles
```

Hyphens are more readable in URLs and are considered the web standard.

5. Avoid Verbs in Resource Names

In REST, **the HTTP method already expresses the action**.
The URL should simply represent the resource.

 Good:

bash
CopyEdit
POST /users
DELETE /users/123

✖ Bad:

bash
CopyEdit
/createUser
/deleteUser/123

Remember: your API should sound like you are operating on nouns, not invoking actions.

6. Use Lowercase Letters

URLs are case-sensitive, and lowercase URLs are simpler and more predictable.

 Good:

bash
CopyEdit
/users
/products

Bad:

CopyEdit
/Users
/Products

Stick to lowercase for consistency and professionalism.

Quick Checklist for Resource Naming

- ■ Plural nouns for collections

- ■ Singular nouns for individual resources

- ■ Hyphens for multi-word names

- ■ No verbs in the URL

- ■ Lowercase only

- ■ Consistency across all endpoints

Getting the naming right makes everything else about your API — documentation, onboarding, usage — dramatically easier.

5.2 Organizing Routes and URL Structures

Good API design isn't just about naming individual endpoints.
It's also about **organizing your routes logically** so that relationships between resources are clear and navigable.

A well-organized route structure:

- Reflects real-world relationships,

- Is predictable,

- Is scalable as the system grows.

Let's explore how to do this correctly.

Organizing by Resource Hierarchy

If a resource naturally belongs under another resource, represent that relationship in the URL.

Example: Orders belonging to Users

bash
CopyEdit
```
/users/123/orders
/users/123/orders/456
```

Here:

- /users/123/orders → List all orders for user 123.

- /users/123/orders/456 → Get details for order 456 placed by user 123.

The URL reflects the logical containment of **orders inside users**.

Use Nesting When It Makes Sense (But Don't Overdo It)

Good Nesting:
Reflects a clear parent-child relationship without excessive complexity.

Example:

bash
CopyEdit
```
/companies/45/employees/123
```

Bad Nesting:
Nesting three, four, or more levels deep makes URLs cumbersome and harder to use.

Example:

```bash
CopyEdit
/schools/10/classes/5/teachers/2/students/20/grades/1
```

■ Best practice:

- Limit nesting to **two or three levels** maximum.

- If it gets deeper, consider flattening the structure or adding query parameters instead.

Flat Structure for Top-Level Resources

Not every piece of data needs to be nested.
Top-level resources should have flat, simple routes.

Examples:

```bash
CopyEdit
/users
/products
/orders
/courses
```

Even if users belong to companies internally, it doesn't mean the frontend must fetch users only through /companies/45/users.
Keep APIs easy to consume unless a relationship is critical.

Use Query Parameters for Filtering and Actions

Avoid inventing weird URL patterns for filtering.
Use standard **query parameters** instead.

Good:

bash
CopyEdit
GET /products?category=books&price_lt=50

❌ Bad:

swift
CopyEdit
GET /products/by-category/books/under-50

Query parameters keep routes clean and flexible.

Standard Action Endpoints

When you need to trigger a **specific action** that doesn't fit cleanly into CRUD operations, you can add a sub-resource or suffix.

Examples:

bash
CopyEdit
POST /users/123/reset-password
POST /orders/456/cancel
POST /products/789/archive

This keeps the noun-based resource model intact while still allowing actions when needed.

Summary: API Routing Golden Rules

- Reflect real-world relationships in URL hierarchy.

- Keep nesting shallow.

- Keep top-level resources flat and simple.

- Use query parameters for filters and searches.

- Clearly separate resource operations from actions.

Organized, clean route structures make APIs **predictable**, **scalable**, and **pleasant to work with**.

5.3 API Versioning Strategies

Even the best-designed API will eventually need to **change** — to fix bugs, improve performance, add new features, or adapt to new requirements.

But here's the catch:
Once an API is released, you cannot assume clients will immediately adapt to changes.
If you change an API without notice, you could break production apps, lose customers, and cause widespread frustration.

That's why **versioning** your API is critical.

What is API Versioning?

API versioning is the practice of **managing changes** to your API without disrupting existing users.
It allows multiple versions of the API to exist at the same time.

New users can use the latest version, while existing users can continue using the version they originally built against.

Why Version Your API?

- **Backward Compatibility:**
  Prevents breaking client apps that rely on old behavior.

- **Smooth Transition:**
  Gives users time to migrate to new versions.

- **Controlled Evolution:**
  Lets you add features, redesign endpoints, or improve security over time.

Without versioning, you would either:

- Freeze your API forever (bad for innovation),

- Or break clients constantly (bad for business).

Neither is acceptable.

Common API Versioning Strategies

There are several ways to introduce versions into your API. Let's review the most common:

1. URI Versioning (Recommended for Beginners)

The version is included directly in the URL.

Example:

```bash
CopyEdit
/api/v1/users
/api/v2/users
```

Advantages:

- Very visible and clear to developers.

- Easy to route requests based on version.

- Easy to maintain separate controllers/services internally.

Disadvantages:

- Changes the URL structure whenever a version updates.

Still, for beginner and intermediate projects, **URI versioning is the most practical** and widely used approach.

2. Header Versioning

The version is specified in the HTTP headers instead of the URL.

Example:

```
http
CopyEdit
Accept: application/vnd.example.v1+json
```

Advantages:

- Clean URLs (no version clutter in the path).

- Flexible for complex versioning strategies.

Disadvantages:

- Harder to discover or guess without good documentation.

- Some tools and proxies may strip or mishandle custom headers.

Header versioning is more common in **large enterprise APIs**.

3. Query Parameter Versioning

The version is passed as a query parameter.

Example:

```bash
CopyEdit
/users?version=1
```

Advantages:

- Easy to implement.

Disadvantages:

- Pollutes query string.

- Looks less clean than other methods.

- Can confuse users and developers.

Query parameter versioning is **less preferred** for modern APIs.

Best Practices for Versioning

- **Start with v1** — even at your first release.

- **Communicate changes** clearly in your documentation.

- **Deprecate old versions** carefully with warnings and timelines.

- **Minimize breaking changes** unless absolutely necessary.

- **Version APIs, not individual resources** — version the entire API behavior.

5.4 Error Handling and Standardized Responses

Building an API isn't just about getting things right when everything goes smoothly. A **truly professional API** is judged by **how well it handles errors** — because in real-world applications, errors are inevitable.

Poor error handling leads to:

- Confused users,

- Hard-to-debug client applications,

- Frustrated developers.

Clear, consistent error handling, on the other hand, makes your API:

- Easier to use,

- Easier to integrate,

- Easier to debug.

Let's dive into how to handle errors the right way.

The Importance of Good Error Responses

When a client sends a bad request, they need to know:

- **What went wrong,**

- **Why it went wrong,**

- **How they can fix it.**

Vague messages like:

javascript
CopyEdit

```
Error 400
```

or

nginx
CopyEdit

```
Something went wrong
```

are useless and infuriating for developers using your API.

A good error response is **predictable, informative**, and **structured**.

Key Components of a Good Error Response

A proper error response should include:

- **HTTP Status Code:** A correct and meaningful code.

- **Error Message:** A human-readable summary of the error.

- **Error Code (Optional):** A machine-readable internal error identifier.

- **Details (Optional):** Specific fields or parameters causing the problem.

- **Timestamp (Optional):** Helpful for debugging logs.

Example of a Professional Error Response:

json
CopyEdit

```
{
  "error": "Validation Failed",
```

```json
"error_code": "VALIDATION_ERROR",
"details": {
  "email": "Email must be a valid format",
  "password": "Password must be at least 8 characters"
},
"status": 400,
"timestamp": "2025-04-25T12:30:45Z"
}
```

- Developers can quickly understand what went wrong,

- Frontend teams can show user-friendly error messages,

- Backend teams can trace the issue with the error code and timestamp.

Standardizing Error Format Across Your API

Once you design an error format you like, **stick to it across your entire API**.

Example Standard Error Format:

json
CopyEdit
```json
{
  "error": "Short human-readable message",
  "error_code": "MACHINE_READABLE_CODE",
  "details": { /* Optional additional information */ },
  "status": 400,
  "timestamp": "ISO8601_TIMESTAMP"
}
```

Consistency is key — developers should never have to guess what structure an error response will have.

Using the Right Status Codes for Errors

Choosing the correct status code improves clarity:

Status Code	Usage Example
400	Malformed or invalid request.
401	Authentication failure (no or invalid token).
403	Authorization failure (permission denied).
404	Resource not found.
409	Conflict (duplicate resource, business rule).
422	Unprocessable Entity (validation failed).
500	Internal server error (unexpected server crash).

Always remember:

- **Client errors** (mistakes in the request) → 400 series.

- **Server errors** (your API's fault) → 500 series.

Helpful Tips for Error Handling

- Return useful errors during validation (e.g., missing fields, wrong data types).

- Avoid leaking sensitive information in error messages (e.g., database internals).

- Log detailed errors internally for debugging but show only safe messages to clients.

- When in doubt, **be generous with details** for developers, but cautious with sensitive data exposure.

A great API doesn't just succeed gracefully — it fails gracefully too.

5.5 Writing Clear and Helpful API Documentation

Even if you build a flawless, world-class API, it won't matter if no one understands how to use it.

API documentation is your API's user manual.

It should answer:

- What endpoints exist?

- What requests are expected?

- What responses will be returned?

- What errors could happen?

- How should authentication work?

Good documentation is not optional — it's a core feature of a professional API.

Why Great Documentation Matters

- **Reduces support requests:**
  Developers can solve problems themselves.

- **Accelerates onboarding:**
  New users or teams can integrate faster.

- **Builds trust:**
  Well-documented APIs are seen as more reliable and serious.

- **Improves adoption:**
  Developers **choose APIs** they can understand quickly.

You want your documentation to be so good that developers actually enjoy using it.

Essential Sections of Good API Documentation

1. **Overview and Introduction**

Provide a short, clear explanation of:

- What the API does,

- Key concepts and terminology,

- How to authenticate.

2. **Authentication Instructions**

Explain:

- What authentication method is used (API keys, OAuth2, etc.),

- How to obtain credentials,

- How to pass credentials in requests (e.g., Authorization: Bearer <token>).

3. **Endpoint Reference**

For each endpoint, include:

- **HTTP Method and URL:**
  e.g., GET /users

- **Description:**
  What this endpoint does.

- **Request Headers:**
  Required or optional headers.

- **Request Parameters:**
  Query parameters or body fields, their types, and whether they are required.

- **Request Body Example (if applicable):**

json
CopyEdit

```
{
  "username": "newuser",
  "email": "newuser@example.com"
}
```

- **Response Example:**

json
CopyEdit

```
{
  "id": 123,
  "username": "newuser",
  "email": "newuser@example.com"
}
```

- **Possible Error Responses:**

  o 400 Bad Request

  o 401 Unauthorized

  o 404 Not Found

Everything should be **predictable and complete**.

4. Common Use Cases and Tutorials

Provide short walkthroughs for:

- How to create a resource,

- How to update a resource,

- How to fetch a filtered list,

- How to handle authentication failures.

Use real examples with actual request and response payloads.
Walk new users through the "happy path" quickly.

5. Error Handling Reference

Document:

- What error structures look like,

- What status codes your API uses,

- How to interpret common errors.

Developers should not be surprised by errors — they should expect them and know how to respond.

6. **Change Log / Version History**

If you publish multiple versions of your API, maintain a **changelog**:

- New features,

- Breaking changes,

- Deprecated endpoints.

This helps existing users plan their upgrades or migrations smoothly.

Best Practices for API Documentation

- **Be specific, not vague.**
  Don't just say "returns data" — show exactly what the response structure looks like.

- **Be concise, not verbose.**
  Keep explanations focused. Long walls of text intimidate developers.

- **Use consistent examples.**
  Stick with a few example resources (like users, products) across the documentation.

- **Provide sample code snippets.**
  For popular languages (e.g., cURL, Python requests, JavaScript fetch).

- **Update the documentation when the API changes.**
  Outdated documentation is worse than no documentation at all.

Tools to Help Write and Maintain API Docs

Modern tools make documentation easier:

- **Swagger / OpenAPI:**
  Write machine-readable API descriptions and auto-generate documentation.

- **Redoc:**
  A clean, professional UI for Swagger/OpenAPI specs.

- **Postman:**
  Great for creating example collections and sharing interactive docs.

- **Stoplight, ReadMe:**
  Platforms for managing full API portals.

Even simple Markdown files in a GitHub repository are better than nothing — just make sure they are clear, structured, and complete.

Chapter 6: Your First API — A Practical Guide

6.1 Setting Up Your Development Environment

Now that you have a solid understanding of how APIs work and how to design them properly, it's time to **roll up your sleeves and build your first API**.

Before you start coding, you need a development environment that is:

- Simple,

- Clean,

- Ready for productivity.

Let's go through setting up your API development environment step-by-step.

Tools You Need

Here are the core tools you'll install:

- **A Code Editor:**
  A text editor with programming support (VS Code is highly recommended).

- **Terminal/Command Line:**
  You'll use the terminal to install packages and run your server.

- **Runtime (Python or Node.js):**
  Depending on your tech stack (we'll choose soon).

- **API Testing Tool:**
  Postman or a lightweight browser extension like Thunder Client (VS Code extension).

- **Version Control System (Optional for now):**
  Git for managing your code versions (not mandatory at the beginning but highly recommended).

Setting Up Your Machine

Step 1: Install Visual Studio Code (VS Code)

- Go to https://code.visualstudio.com/.

- Download and install it for your operating system (Windows, Mac, Linux).

VS Code is powerful yet lightweight and has built-in extensions for Python, Node.js, Git, and even API testing.

Step 2: Install Python or Node.js

Depending on the tech stack you'll choose (covered in 6.2), install:

- **Python:**
  Download and install from https://python.org/downloads/. Make sure to check **"Add Python to PATH"** during installation.

- **Node.js:**
  Download and install from https://nodejs.org/en/download/.

Both come with package managers built-in:

- **pip** (Python's package manager),

- **npm** (Node.js package manager).

Step 3: Install Postman

- Go to https://postman.com/.

- Download and install Postman for your system.

Alternatively, if you prefer something lightweight:

- Install **Thunder Client** extension inside VS Code.

Both tools allow you to send API requests easily without writing client-side code manually.

Step 4: Create a Dedicated Workspace

Inside your computer:

- Create a folder named something like api-practice or first-api-project.

- Inside this folder, you'll organize your project files.

Keeping a clean workspace makes it easier to manage projects, especially as they grow.

Final Quick Checklist

Before moving forward, confirm you have:

- VS Code installed,

- Python or Node.js installed,

- Postman (or Thunder Client) ready,

- A project folder created.

■ Now you're ready to choose your tech stack and build your first real API.

6.2 Choosing Your First Tech Stack (Python Flask or Node.js Express)

Choosing a tech stack can feel overwhelming for beginners.
 Luckily, for your **first API**, you only need to choose between **two excellent beginner-friendly options**:

- **Python Flask**

- **Node.js Express**

Both are lightweight, easy to set up, and widely used professionally.
 Let's quickly compare them so you can pick the one that suits you.

Option 1: Python Flask

Flask is a micro web framework for Python, meaning:

- It's simple,

- It's minimal,

- It doesn't force you into rigid patterns.

Why Choose Flask?

- If you're more comfortable with Python,

- If you want readable, beginner-friendly code,

- If you plan to later integrate with data science, machine learning, or backend systems.

Key Features:

- Very lightweight (minimal setup),

- Easy to create REST APIs,

- Excellent documentation,

- Lots of community support.

Option 2: Node.js Express

Express is a minimal web framework for Node.js (JavaScript runtime), known for:

- Speed,

- Simplicity,

- Massive ecosystem of libraries.

Why Choose Express?

- If you're more comfortable with JavaScript,

- If you want to move into full-stack web development (especially React, Vue, Angular),

- If you're thinking about serverless, real-time apps later.

Key Features:

- Simple to build REST APIs,

- Rich middleware system (easy to extend),

- Huge community and package ecosystem,

- Runs everywhere JavaScript runs.

How to Decide?

Factor	Choose Flask if...	Choose Express if...
Language	You prefer Python.	You prefer JavaScript.
Future Interests	Backend APIs, data science.	Full-stack web apps, serverless apps.
Simplicity for Beginners	Very beginner-friendly.	Slightly more configuration needed.
Ecosystem	Python packages.	NPM ecosystem.

Important:
There's no wrong choice.
Both Flask and Express will teach you the exact API fundamentals you need.

Pick the one that aligns better with your comfort level or career interests, and let's start building.

(For this book, examples will show **both options** side-by-side whenever necessary.)

6.3 Building Your First Simple REST API (Step-by-Step)

Now, it's time to **build your very first REST API**.
We'll create a simple **"Users" API** that can:

- Get a list of users,

- Add a new user.

You'll be amazed at how quickly you can build a working API once you have the environment ready.

Let's walk through it carefully.

Step 1: Initialize Your Project

Create a folder for your project:

```sql
CopyEdit
first-api-project/
```

Open it in VS Code.

If Using Python + Flask:

Create a new Python file, e.g., app.py.

Install Flask via pip:

```bash
CopyEdit
pip install flask
```

If Using Node.js + Express:

Initialize a Node project:

```bash
CopyEdit
npm init -y
```

Install Express:

```bash
CopyEdit
npm install express
```

Create a file named app.js.

Step 2: Set Up Your API Server

Basic Flask Server:

```python
CopyEdit
# app.py
from flask import Flask, jsonify, request

app = Flask(__name__)
```

```python
# In-memory "database"
users = []

@app.route('/users', methods=['GET'])
def get_users():
    return jsonify(users)

@app.route('/users', methods=['POST'])
def add_user():
    data = request.get_json()
    users.append(data)
    return jsonify(data), 201

if __name__ == '__main__':
    app.run(debug=True)
```

Basic Express Server:

javascript
CopyEdit

```javascript
// app.js
const express = require('express');
const app = express();

app.use(express.json());

// In-memory "database"
const users = [];

app.get('/users', (req, res) => {
  res.json(users);
});

app.post('/users', (req, res) => {
  users.push(req.body);
  res.status(201).json(req.body);
});
```

```
app.listen(3000, () => {
  console.log('Server running on port 3000');
});
```

Step 3: Run Your API

In Python:

```bash
CopyEdit
python app.py
```

- Flask will start the server, usually at http://127.0.0.1:5000/.

In Node.js:

```bash
CopyEdit
node app.js
```

- Express will start the server, usually at http://localhost:3000/.

You'll see a message like "Running on http://127.0.0.1:5000/" (Flask) or "Server running on port 3000" (Express).

■ Your API is now live on your machine!

Step 4: Test Your API

Use Postman or Thunder Client to test:

1. **GET users**

- Method: GET

- URL: http://localhost:5000/users (Flask)
  or http://localhost:3000/users (Express)

- Should return an empty array [] initially.

2. **POST a new user**

- Method: POST

- URL: http://localhost:5000/users **(Flask)**
  or http://localhost:3000/users **(Express)**

- Body (JSON):

json
CopyEdit
```
{
 "id": 1,
 "name": "Alice"
}
```

- Should return the newly added user and status code 201 Created.

3. **GET users again**

Now, calling GET /users should return:

json
CopyEdit
```
[
 {
  "id": 1,
  "name": "Alice"
 }
]
```

You've officially built a working REST API!

108

Step 5: Celebrate (You Deserve It)

At this point:

- You've set up your environment,

- You've picked a tech stack,

- You've built a functioning API that handles GET and POST requests.

This is a huge milestone.
 You now understand firsthand how simple and powerful API development can be.

From here, we'll keep expanding this foundation — adding more features, handling errors properly, securing your API, and making it production-ready.

You're no longer just reading about APIs.
 You're building them.

6.4 Testing Locally with Postman or Curl

Once you've built your first basic API, testing becomes the next critical skill.
 Testing ensures that:

- Your API works as expected,

- Errors are caught early,

- You can confidently build more complex features later.

While you can technically test an API by writing client-side code, it's much faster and easier to use tools specifically made for testing — like Postman or curl.

Let's walk through how to use both.

Testing with Postman

Postman is a free and popular tool that lets you send HTTP requests without writing code.

It's like having a full client application at your fingertips — ideal for testing APIs during development.

Step 1: Install Postman

- Download from https://postman.com/downloads/.

- Install and open it.

Step 2: Sending a Simple GET Request

1. Open Postman.

2. Click "New" → "HTTP Request."

3. Set the method to GET.

4. Enter your API URL:

   ○ **For Flask:** http://localhost:5000/users

   ○ **For Express:** http://localhost:3000/users

5. **Click "Send."**

■ You should see a response:

json

CopyEdit

[]

(or a list of users if you already added one).

Postman shows you:

- Response status code (e.g., 200 OK),

- Response time,

- Response body (JSON).

Step 3: Sending a POST Request

1. Change the method to POST.

2. Use the same URL: /users.

3. Go to the "Body" tab → Select "raw" → Choose "JSON" format.

4. Enter JSON data:

json

CopyEdit

```
{
  "id": 2,
  "name": "Bob"
}
```

5. Click "Send."

You should see a 201 Created response with the user object.

Now, doing another GET should return both Alice and Bob!

111

Step 4: Checking Errors

Try sending incomplete or wrong data:

json

CopyEdit

```
{

  "username": "Charlie"

}
```

See how your API responds — this will help you plan better error handling.

Postman helps you catch mistakes before users do.

Testing with Curl (Command Line)

If you prefer (or need) to work from the terminal, curl is a quick way to send HTTP requests.

Example: GET Users

bash

CopyEdit

```
curl http://localhost:5000/users
```

or

bash

CopyEdit

```
curl http://localhost:3000/users
```

Example: POST New User

bash

CopyEdit

```
curl -X POST http://localhost:5000/users -H "Content-Type: application/json" -d
'{"id":3, "name":"Charlie"}'
```

or

bash

CopyEdit

```
curl -X POST http://localhost:3000/users -H "Content-Type: application/json" -d
'{"id":3, "name":"Charlie"}'
```

- -X POST specifies the method.

- -H sets the header (Content-Type: application/json).

- -d sends the JSON data.

■ You'll see the JSON response right in your terminal.

Why Test Locally Before Deploying?

- Catch errors early.

- Validate input handling.

- Check correct status codes.

- Confirm JSON structure.

- Ensure server stability.

Building confidence early saves massive amounts of frustration later.

6.5 Common Mistakes to Avoid in Your First API

As a beginner API developer, it's easy to make certain mistakes — everyone does at first.
What separates great developers from average ones is learning to avoid (or quickly fix) these early traps.

Let's look at the most common beginner mistakes — and how you can avoid them.

1. Not Using Proper HTTP Status Codes

Returning 200 OK for everything — even for errors — is one of the fastest ways to confuse users.

Always use:

- 201 Created for successful POSTs,

- 400 Bad Request for invalid inputs,

- 404 Not Found when resource doesn't exist,

- 500 Internal Server Error for server-side problems.

Clients depend on status codes to know what happened.

2. Forgetting to Validate Incoming Data

Beginners often assume that clients will send perfect data.
Reality check: They won't.

■ Always:

- Validate required fields (e.g., name, email),

- Check data types,

- Enforce formats (e.g., email must be valid),

- Handle missing or malformed JSON.

Example (Flask):

python

CopyEdit

```
if not 'name' in data:
    return jsonify({"error": "Missing name field"}), 400
```

Example (Express):

javascript

CopyEdit

```
if (!req.body.name) {
    return res.status(400).json({ error: "Missing name field" });
}
```

Bad data should trigger clear, useful errors.

3. Ignoring Error Handling

Some beginners only code for "happy paths" — where everything works perfectly.

■ Always:

- Anticipate failures (e.g., database down, invalid input),

- Catch exceptions,

- Return helpful error responses.

Example in Flask:

python

CopyEdit

```python
try:
    users.append(data)
except Exception as e:
    return jsonify({"error": str(e)}), 500
```

Example in Express:

javascript

CopyEdit

```javascript
try {
  users.push(req.body);
} catch (error) {
  res.status(500).json({ error: error.message });
```

Handling errors gracefully is a sign of professional development.

4. Hardcoding Data Without Future Consideration

In early demos, you might hardcode users into a simple list or array.
That's okay for learning — but in production, you should always connect to a real database.

When moving beyond basics:

- Start using lightweight databases like SQLite, MongoDB, or PostgreSQL.

- Avoid hardcoded data for any long-term project.

Hardcoded data = no persistence.
When the server restarts, all data vanishes.

5. Not Structuring Project Files Properly

Throwing all your code into one giant file (app.py, app.js) works at first but quickly becomes unmanageable.

Even small projects benefit from structure:

- Separate routes, controllers, services, and models.

- Organize files into folders like /routes, /controllers, /models.

Good project structure = easier maintenance, collaboration, and scaling.

6. Forgetting About Security

Even beginner APIs need basic security measures:

- Always use HTTPS when moving to production.

- Validate and sanitize all inputs to avoid injections.

- Require authentication for sensitive routes.

Security is not an afterthought — it's a habit.
Start practicing it early.

Chapter 7: Testing and Debugging Your API Like a Pro

7.1 Introduction to API Testing Tools (Postman, Thunder Client)

Building your API is only the first step.
 Ensuring it actually works — reliably, under real conditions — is what separates **hobby projects** from **professional-grade applications**.

That's where **API testing** comes in.

Instead of building complex frontend apps just to test your backend, you can use specialized **API testing tools** that let you send requests, inspect responses, simulate edge cases, and catch bugs early.

The two best tools to start with are:

- **Postman** (standalone app),

- **Thunder Client** (VS Code extension).

Let's walk through both.

Postman: The Industry Standard

Postman is a full-featured API development environment.

Key features:

- Send requests (GET, POST, PUT, DELETE) easily,

- Organize endpoints into Collections,

- Save and reuse test cases,

- Write automated tests (basic scripts),

- Manage environments (local, staging, production),

- Share APIs with teams.

Postman Strengths:

- Very user-friendly UI,

- Powerful scripting options,

- Supports authentication (API keys, OAuth2, Bearer tokens),

- Excellent for both manual and automated API testing,

- Free for individuals and small teams.

If you're serious about APIs — whether building them or consuming them — **learning Postman is almost mandatory**.

Thunder Client: Lightweight and Fast

Thunder Client is a VS Code extension designed for developers who prefer to stay inside their code editor.

Key features:

- Send requests directly from VS Code,

- Simple UI for basic testing,

- Lightweight and fast (no heavyweight app),

- Basic Collections and environment management.

Thunder Client Strengths:

- Blazing fast startup (no separate app needed),

- Great for quick tests during active development,

- Minimal distractions.

While not as powerful as Postman in terms of advanced scripting and team collaboration, **Thunder Client is perfect for day-to-day API development work**.

Which Tool Should You Use?

Use Case	Postman	Thunder Client
Complex testing & automation	Best choice	Basic support
Working inside VS Code	Possible with extensions	Built-in and seamless
Lightweight quick testing	Slightly heavier	Extremely fast and lightweight

Tip:
Use Thunder Client for quick local development testing, and Postman when you need full testing suites, API docs, or environment switching.

7.2 Writing Basic Test Cases for Your Endpoints

After setting up your testing tool, the next professional step is to **write basic test cases** for each API endpoint you create.

A test case is simply a **defined scenario**:

- What you send,

- What you expect to receive.

Good API developers write **basic tests first** — not just when something goes wrong later.

What Should a Basic API Test Cover?

For each endpoint, test:

1. **Successful Responses**

    ○ Correct data returned.

    ○ Correct status code (e.g., 200, 201).

2. **Failure Cases**

    ○ Missing fields (should trigger 400 error).

    ○ Unauthorized access (should trigger 401).

    ○ Resource not found (should trigger 404).

3. **Data Integrity**

    ○ Data types are correct (e.g., ID is a number, name is a string).

    ○ Fields returned match the expected structure.

Example: Testing a POST /users Endpoint

Test Case 1: Successful User Creation

- Send valid user data.

- Expect 201 Created response.

- Expect user object in the response body.

Test Case 2: Missing Required Field

- Send JSON without a name.

- Expect 400 Bad Request response.

- Expect error message about missing name.

Test Case 3: Unauthorized Access (if applicable)

- Send request without API token.

- Expect 401 Unauthorized response.

How to Write a Basic Test in Postman

Postman lets you **write scripts** inside the "Tests" tab of each request.

Example (checking for a 201 status code):

javascript
CopyEdit
```
pm.test("Status code is 201", function () {
    pm.response.to.have.status(201);
});
```

Example (checking if response has id field):

javascript
CopyEdit
```
pm.test("Response should have user ID", function () {
    var jsonData = pm.response.json();
    pm.expect(jsonData.id).to.exist;
});
```

Writing even a few small tests saves you from manual re-checking — and helps you catch regressions automatically later.

7.3 Automating API Testing with Scripts

After writing basic manual tests, you can take your skills up a notch by **automating** your API testing with **scripts**.

Automated tests mean:

- **Faster feedback**: know immediately if something breaks,

- **Better consistency**: run the same tests every time,

- **Less manual effort**: save your brainpower for building, not rechecking.

Postman Collection Runner

One easy way to automate tests is using Postman's **Collection Runner**.

Step-by-Step:

1. Group related API requests into a **Collection** (e.g., "User API Tests").

2. Write tests under the "Tests" tab for each request.

3. Open the Collection Runner.

4. Run all requests automatically.

5. See a full report: which tests passed, which failed.

You can simulate full workflows:

- Create a user,

- Fetch the user,

- Update the user,

- Delete the user.

All with one click.

Writing Multiple Assertions

You can chain multiple assertions in a single test.

Example:

javascript
CopyEdit

```
pm.test("User creation success", function () {
    pm.response.to.have.status(201);

    var data = pm.response.json();
    pm.expect(data).to.have.property('id');
    pm.expect(data.name).to.eql("Alice");
});
```

This checks:

- Correct status,

- Presence of ID,

- Correct name field value.

Bonus Tip: Environment Variables

Use Postman **Environments** to:

- Store base URLs (local, staging, production),

- Save tokens after login requests,

- Dynamically reuse values (like user IDs between requests).

This makes your tests much more powerful and flexible.

7.4 Debugging Common API Issues

Even after careful building and testing, **errors will happen** — especially early on.

Professional developers aren't those who never encounter bugs; they're the ones who **find and fix bugs efficiently**.

Let's talk about **common API problems** — and how to debug them.

1. 404 Not Found

Problem:

- Wrong endpoint URL,

- Wrong HTTP method,

- Missing route in your server code.

How to Debug:

- Double-check your route names and methods (case-sensitive).

- Verify if the route is actually registered.

- Ensure you're hitting the correct server URL/port.

2. 400 Bad Request

Problem:

- Malformed JSON,

- Missing required fields,

- Wrong Content-Type header.

126

How to Debug:

- Validate your request body against expected structure.

- Always set Content-Type: application/json for JSON APIs.

- Use Postman's "Pretty" view to confirm request format.

3. 401 Unauthorized

Problem:

- Missing or invalid authentication credentials.

How to Debug:

- Ensure you send Authorization headers.

- Check token validity.

- Confirm the server is expecting the right authentication method.

4. 500 Internal Server Error

Problem:

- Server-side code crash,

- Uncaught exception,

- Database or service connection failure.

How to Debug:

- Check server logs for traceback or error stack.

- Add error-handling middleware or try/except blocks.

- Log the error messages for investigation.

In Flask:

```python
CopyEdit
app.logger.error('Something went wrong', exc_info=True)
```

In Express:

```javascript
CopyEdit
app.use((err, req, res, next) => {
  console.error(err.stack);
  res.status(500).send('Something broke!');
});
```

5. Incorrect Data Returned

Problem:

- Mistakes in query logic,

- Bad mappings,

- Mismatched field names.

How to Debug:

- Inspect your data flow carefully.

- Add logging at key points (before returning response).

- Compare expected vs. actual data structures.

Chapter 8: Securing Your API

8.1 Why API Security Matters

Building a powerful API is important.
But building a secure API is absolutely critical.

APIs are gateways into your system — they can expose sensitive data, trigger financial transactions, manage user accounts, and much more.
If your API isn't secured properly, you're not just risking your own application — you're potentially endangering your users, their data, and your organization's reputation.

Real-World Risks of Poor API Security

- **Data Breaches:**
  Personal, financial, or confidential data could be leaked or stolen.

- **Account Hijacking:**
  Unauthorized users could take over accounts by exploiting weak endpoints.

- **Service Downtime:**
  Attackers could flood your API with requests, bringing your service down (Denial of Service attacks).

- **Financial Loss:**
  If your API controls transactions, fraudsters could exploit vulnerabilities to steal money or resources.

- **Reputational Damage:**
  News of an API breach spreads fast, destroying trust in your brand.

In short:

If you build an API, securing it is your responsibility.

Luckily, basic API security concepts are straightforward once you understand them — and small steps can make a big difference.

8.2 Introduction to API Keys and Basic Authentication

One of the first and simplest forms of securing an API is using **API Keys** or **Basic Authentication**.

Let's understand what these are — and when to use them.

API Keys

An **API Key** is a **unique identifier** sent along with each API request.
It acts like a password that authenticates the client calling your API.

How API Keys Work:

- The client (application) is given a key (e.g., abc123xyz).

- The client includes the key in each request, usually in a header or query parameter.

- The server checks if the key is valid before processing the request.

Example: Using API Key in Header

Request Header:

makefile
CopyEdit
Authorization: ApiKey abc123xyz

Or sometimes in query parameters:

bash
CopyEdit
GET /users?api_key=abc123xyz

When to Use API Keys:

- For **identifying** applications or users (not securing highly sensitive data).

- For **rate limiting** (e.g., limiting users to 1000 requests/day).

- For **internal APIs** or services not handling sensitive personal data.

Limitations of API Keys:

- API Keys can be stolen if not used over HTTPS.

- They don't provide information about who the user is — only which app is calling.

- They should not be considered strong authentication for user-specific data.

Thus, API Keys are **good for basic security**, but not sufficient alone for serious protection.

Basic Authentication

Basic Auth is another simple method where:

- The client sends a **username** and **password** with every API request.

- These credentials are encoded (not encrypted) using Base64.

Request Header Example:

makefile
CopyEdit
Authorization: Basic dXNlcm5hbWU6cGFzc3dvcmQ=

Decoded, this Base64 string means:

makefile

132

When to Use Basic Auth:

- Very small, internal APIs,

- Quick prototyping,

- Cases where encryption is guaranteed (i.e., HTTPS is enforced).

Limitations of Basic Auth:

- Very insecure if used without HTTPS.

- Credentials are static (same every time).

- Not scalable for larger systems.

Thus, **Basic Auth is outdated for most production systems** — better options like **tokens** exist today.

8.3 Understanding Tokens and JWT (Beginner-Friendly)

For modern, scalable, secure APIs, **token-based authentication** has become the standard.
 And the most popular token format today is the **JWT** — JSON Web Token.

Let's explain it simply.

133

What is a Token?

A **token** is a **small piece of data** that proves you are authenticated.

Instead of sending your username and password on every request, you:

1. Log in once with username/password,

2. The server gives you a token,

3. You send the token with every future API request.

Tokens are **temporary**, **revocable**, and **safer** than sending credentials repeatedly.

What is a JWT (JSON Web Token)?

A **JWT** is a specific kind of token — it's just a **compact, self-contained string** containing:

- Information about the user (claims),

- A signature to ensure it wasn't tampered with.

A JWT looks like this:

CopyEdit
```
eyJhbGciOiJIUzI1NiIsInR5cCI6IkpXVCJ9.
eyJ1c2VybmFtZSI6ImFsaWNlIiwiaWQiOjEyM30.
dBjftJeZ4CVP-mB92K27uhbUJU1p1r_wW1gFWFOEjXk
```

It has three parts:

- **Header** (metadata like algorithm used),

- **Payload** (actual user info, e.g., ID, username),

- **Signature** (to verify authenticity).

How JWT Authentication Works:

1. User logs in (POST /login) → Server validates credentials.

2. Server creates a JWT token and sends it back to the client.

3. Client stores the token (e.g., in localStorage, or an app variable).

4. Client sends the token in the Authorization header for future requests:

makefile
CopyEdit
Authorization: Bearer <your_jwt_token>

5. Server validates the token and processes the request if it's valid.

Benefits of JWTs:

- No need to store sessions server-side (stateless authentication).

- Faster authentication on each request.

- Easy to scale across multiple servers.

Important Reminder:
Always use **HTTPS** when using JWTs to prevent token theft over the network!

8.4 Rate Limiting: Protecting Your API from Abuse

Even with authentication, APIs are vulnerable to:

- **Spam requests,**

- **Brute-force attacks,**

- **Accidental infinite loops.**

Rate limiting is the practice of **restricting how many requests a client can make** over a period of time.

Why Rate Limiting Matters

- **Prevents Abuse:** Stops users from flooding your servers intentionally or accidentally.

- **Improves Stability:** Ensures fair usage of server resources.

- **Protects APIs from Downtime:** Helps defend against basic denial-of-service (DoS) attacks.

How Rate Limiting Works

You define limits like:

- **100 requests per minute per user,**

- **1000 requests per day per API key,**

- **10 login attempts per hour.**

If a client exceeds the limit:

- The server responds with 429 Too Many Requests.

Example response:

```json
CopyEdit
{
  "error": "Too many requests. Try again later.",
```

```
"status": 429
}
```

Implementing Rate Limiting (Overview)

- **In Flask:** Use Flask-Limiter package.

- **In Express:** Use express-rate-limit middleware.

Example (Node.js with Express):

```javascript
CopyEdit
const rateLimit = require('express-rate-limit');

const limiter = rateLimit({
  windowMs: 15 * 60 * 1000, // 15 minutes
  max: 100 // limit each IP to 100 requests per windowMs
});

app.use(limiter);
```

Simple but extremely effective!

8.5 CORS, HTTPS, and Basic Security Configurations

Securing your API is not just about who accesses it — it's also about how it's accessed.

Three final pieces of basic API security:

CORS (Cross-Origin Resource Sharing)

Problem:
Modern browsers **block API requests from different domains** for security reasons.

Example:

- Your API is at api.example.com,

- Your frontend app is at app.example.com.

By default, the browser **won't allow frontend code to call the backend**.

Solution:
You must explicitly allow cross-origin requests using CORS policies.

In Flask:

```python
CopyEdit
from flask_cors import CORS
CORS(app)
```

In Express:

```javascript
CopyEdit
const cors = require('cors');
app.use(cors());
```

■ Now your frontend can interact with your backend safely.

Important:
Always configure CORS carefully — don't just allow all origins (*) in sensitive APIs.

HTTPS: Always Secure the Transport

Never expose APIs over plain HTTP in production.

HTTPS:

- Encrypts requests and responses,

- Prevents eavesdropping,

- Protects tokens, API keys, and user data.

Today, services like Let's Encrypt make HTTPS certificates free and easy to install. **No excuses. Always use HTTPS.**

Other Basic Security Tips

- **Validate inputs** (never trust external data blindly).

- **Return minimal error details** (hide internal server errors from users).

- **Implement API Gateway or WAF** if scaling up (for enterprise-level protection).

- **Rotate API keys and tokens** periodically.

Security is an **ongoing process**, not a one-time setup.

Chapter 9: Pagination, Filtering, and Sorting

9.1 Handling Large Data Sets Efficiently

As your API grows and starts handling real-world data, you'll quickly encounter a critical reality:
Most clients don't want or need all your data at once.

Imagine if a mobile app had to download 100,000 users or 10,000 products in a single API call.
It would be:

- Slow,

- Unreliable,

- Frustrating for users.

Professional APIs handle large data sets **efficiently** by offering:

- **Pagination** (breaking data into manageable chunks),

- **Filtering** (returning only relevant data),

- **Sorting** (controlling the order of returned data).

These techniques make APIs:

- Faster,

- Easier to use,

- Cheaper to operate.

Handling large datasets smartly is a **must-have skill** for any serious API developer.

Why You Should Never Return Everything at Once

- **Performance:**
  Smaller responses mean faster load times and less server load.

- **Mobile Friendliness:**
  Mobile devices have slower networks and limited memory.

- **User Experience:**
  Users typically only need a small part of your full database at any time.

- **Security:**
  Limiting data exposure reduces attack surfaces.

Bottom line:

> **Always assume that APIs should return limited, specific slices of data unless requested otherwise.**

9.2 Designing Pagination (Offset, Cursor-Based)

Pagination allows clients to **retrieve data in chunks,** rather than getting everything at once.

There are two common styles of pagination:

- **Offset-based Pagination** (classic approach),

- **Cursor-based Pagination** (modern, scalable approach).

Let's break down both.

Offset-Based Pagination

Definition:
You specify an **offset** (how many items to skip) and a **limit** (how many items to return).

Example Request:

pgsql
CopyEdit
GET /products?offset=0&limit=10

Returns the first 10 products.

pgsql
CopyEdit
GET /products?offset=10&limit=10

Returns the next 10 products (items 11–20).

Advantages:

- Easy to understand.

- Works well for small-to-medium datasets.

Disadvantages:

- Slow for very large datasets (e.g., skipping millions of rows).

- Data inconsistencies can happen if items are added/removed while paginating.

Cursor-Based Pagination

Definition:
Instead of using offsets, you use a **cursor** (an identifier like a timestamp, ID, or token) to fetch the next page of results.

Example Request:

```sql
GET /products?cursor=158830123
```

Fetch products after item with ID 158830123.

Server responds with:

- Results,

- A new cursor pointing to the last item returned.

Client then uses that cursor for the next page.

Advantages:

- Much faster and more efficient on large datasets.

- No skipping — just picking up where you left off.

- Handles insertions and deletions gracefully.

Disadvantages:

- Slightly more complex to implement.

- Harder for users to jump to arbitrary pages (like page 10).

How to Decide?

Use Case	Recommendation
Small or simple data	Offset pagination
Large or constantly changing data	Cursor pagination

143

Tip:
Start simple (offset) but learn cursor-based techniques early — they're essential for scalable APIs.

9.3 Implementing Filtering and Search Parameters

While pagination helps users navigate large datasets, **filtering** helps users find the right subset of data they actually care about.

Filtering is about providing options to **narrow down results** based on specific criteria.

Common Filtering Techniques

- Filter by **category** (e.g., ?category=books).

- Filter by **date** (e.g., ?created_after=2024-01-01).

- Filter by **status** (e.g., ?status=active).

- Filter by **price range** (e.g., ?price_min=10&price_max=100).

Filtering is **optional** — clients choose when and how to apply filters.

Example of a Filtered Request
bash
CopyEdit
```
GET /products?category=electronics&price_min=100&price_max=500
```

This request:

- Fetches products in the "electronics" category,

- Where the price is between $100 and $500.

Best Practices for Filtering

- **Allow multiple filters to be combined** (e.g., category + price).

- **Validate and sanitize filter inputs** to avoid SQL injection or logical errors.

- **Use clear, predictable query parameter names.**

- **Return meaningful error messages** if filters are invalid.

Implementing Search

Search is like free-text filtering:

- Users search by keywords across fields (e.g., product name, description).

Example:

sql
CopyEdit
GET /products?search=wireless

Returns products that have "wireless" in their name or description.

Tip:
Full-text search is often **harder than simple filtering**, especially for large datasets.
Start with basic LIKE matching, then move toward tools like Elasticsearch if needed later.

9.4 Sorting API Responses Properly

Users often want to **control the order** in which data is returned.

Sorting allows clients to:

- See newest items first,

145

- View products by highest rating,

- Sort users alphabetically, etc.

How to Allow Sorting in Your API

Use query parameters like:

- sort_by

- order

Example Request:

sql
CopyEdit
GET /products?sort_by=price&order=asc

Returns products sorted by ascending price.

pgsql
CopyEdit
GET /users?sort_by=name&order=desc

Returns users sorted by descending name (Z → A).

Default Sort Orders

If the client doesn't specify a sort order:

- Default to something logical and useful (e.g., newest first, alphabetically by name).

Tip:
Document your default sort behaviors clearly in your API documentation.

Sorting Best Practices

- **Allow multiple sorting options** (e.g., sort by price, name, date).

- **Support both ascending and descending orders** (asc, desc).

- **Validate requested sort fields** (prevent errors and security risks).

If a client asks to sort_by=unknownfield, your API should return a **400 Bad Request** — not crash.

Combining Pagination + Filtering + Sorting

In real-world APIs, clients often use **all three** together.

Example:

```
pgsql
CopyEdit
GET
/products?category=books&price_min=10&sort_by=rating&order=desc&offset=0&limit=10
```

This request means:

- Fetch books,

- Costing at least $10,

- Sorted by highest rating first,

- Returning the first 10 results.

Combining these features professionally is what makes your API **powerful** and **pleasant to use**.

Chapter 10: API Performance and Caching Essentials

10.1 Why Performance Matters

When building APIs, developers often focus first on functionality — making sure endpoints work, data is correct, and error handling is robust.
However, a **critical second layer** of professional API development is **performance**.

Performance is not just a technical detail.
It directly affects:

- **User experience,**

- **Business success,**

- **Operational costs.**

Let's explore why performance matters deeply.

How API Performance Impacts Real-World Applications

- **Speed Drives User Satisfaction:**
  Studies show that users expect a response in under **1 second**.
  If your app feels sluggish because of a slow API, users get frustrated — and often leave.

- **Fast APIs Scale Better:**
  A highly efficient API can handle more users with the same infrastructure, saving costs on servers and databases.

- **Performance Affects Business Metrics:**
  Faster APIs lead to higher engagement, better conversion rates, and higher revenue in commercial apps.

- **Search Engine Optimization (SEO):**
  Google's ranking factors now consider page and API performance for web apps.

- **Competitive Advantage:**
  In industries like finance, gaming, and e-commerce, milliseconds matter —
  faster APIs can give your app a serious edge.

What "Good Performance" Means for APIs

Generally:

- **Response times under 200ms** for small/simple requests are excellent.

- **Under 1 second** for large/complex requests is acceptable.

- **Consistency** matters — occasional spikes in latency hurt trust.

Performance isn't just about raw speed. It's about:

- **Consistency,**

- **Scalability under load,**

- **Efficient use of resources.**

Key Factors Affecting API Performance

- Database query speed,

- Server processing time,

- Network latency,

- Size of the payload (response body),

- Backend architecture (caching, database indexing).

Understanding and optimizing these factors is what elevates your API from "works okay" to "works beautifully."

10.2 Introduction to Caching Techniques (Client-side and Server-side)

One of the **most effective ways to boost API performance** is through **caching**.

Caching simply means:

> **Storing copies of expensive data temporarily so you don't have to recompute or refetch it every time.**

Imagine asking for the weather forecast.

- The server looks it up once,

- Stores the result for 10 minutes,

- Serves that cached result for all users during that time,

- Saves work, bandwidth, and time.

Types of Caching

There are two primary types of caching you should understand:

1. Client-Side Caching

In client-side caching:

- The **client** (browser, app) stores the API response.

- Future requests are served from the **client's local cache** instead of asking the server again.

How it works:

- Server includes cache instructions in the HTTP response headers.

- The client obeys these instructions (e.g., cache for 10 minutes).

Common HTTP Headers:

- Cache-Control: public, max-age=600 (cache for 600 seconds),

- ETag (unique identifier for a resource version),

- Last-Modified (timestamp of last change).

Client-side caching **reduces server load** and **makes apps feel lightning-fast**.

2. Server-Side Caching

In server-side caching:

- The **API server** stores the results of expensive operations (e.g., database queries).

- When the same request comes in again, it returns the cached response without reprocessing.

Common types of server caches:

- **In-memory caches** (e.g., Redis, Memcached),

- **Application-layer caches** (simple dictionaries/objects for lightweight caching),

- **Database query result caches.**

Server-side caching improves **performance**, **reduces database strain**, and **lowers latency**.

Caching Strategy Tips

- Cache **read-heavy** endpoints (e.g., GET requests for product listings, articles).

- **Don't cache sensitive or highly dynamic data** (e.g., user profile edits, bank account balances).

- Always set **reasonable expiration times** (TTL — time to live).

Caching is one of your most powerful performance tools — **use it wisely, not recklessly**.

10.3 Adding Simple Caching to Your APIs

Let's get practical:
How can you add **basic caching** to your APIs easily?

You don't need complex tools at first.
Simple in-memory or header-based caching can work wonders.

Here's how.

1. Setting Cache-Control Headers (Client-Side)

You can manually set headers to tell clients how long they can cache responses.

Example in Flask:

```python
CopyEdit
from flask import Flask, jsonify, make_response

app = Flask(__name__)

@app.route('/products')
def get_products():
    response = make_response(jsonify(products))
    response.headers['Cache-Control'] = 'public, max-age=300'  # 5 minutes
    return response
```

Example in Express:

javascript
CopyEdit
```javascript
app.get('/products', (req, res) => {
  res.set('Cache-Control', 'public, max-age=300');
  res.json(products);
});
```

■ Now browsers and API clients will cache the /products response for 5 minutes.

2. Adding Simple In-Memory Server Caching

For lightweight server-side caching, you can temporarily store data in memory.

Example in Flask:

python
CopyEdit
```python
from functools import lru_cache

@lru_cache(maxsize=32)
def get_expensive_data():
    # Simulate heavy computation
    return {'data': 'result'}
```

Example in Express (with simple in-memory caching):

javascript
CopyEdit
```javascript
let cachedData = null;
let cacheTime = 0;

app.get('/expensive', (req, res) => {
  if (cachedData && (Date.now() - cacheTime < 300000)) { // 5 minutes
    return res.json(cachedData);
  }
```

153

```
const data = { result: 'expensive result' }; // Simulated computation
cachedData = data;
cacheTime = Date.now();
res.json(data);
});
```

■ This saves heavy operations by serving cached responses when appropriate.

3. Using Real Cache Engines (Next Level)

When scaling up, use real cache servers like:

- **Redis** (blazing fast, production-ready),

- **Memcached** (lightweight key-value store).

These require installation and integration but provide **huge** performance gains.

Caching Best Practices

- Always **expire cache** after reasonable times.

- Allow clients to force-refresh if needed (e.g., no-cache header).

- Be mindful of **data staleness** risks.

- Cache **only GET** requests, not POST, PUT, DELETE (because those change data).

10.4 Monitoring API Performance

Building a fast API is great.
But **maintaining** speed as your app grows is even more important.

That's where **performance monitoring** comes in.

Why Monitor API Performance?

- Detect slow endpoints before users complain,

- Spot trends (e.g., database queries getting slower),

- Alert on critical issues (e.g., server timeouts, crashes),

- Help prioritize optimizations based on real data.

Professional developers **don't guess performance** — they **measure it**.

Key Metrics to Monitor

- **Response Time:**
  Average time taken to serve requests.

- **Error Rate:**
  How many requests are failing (e.g., 5xx errors).

- **Request Throughput:**
  How many requests your API handles per second/minute.

- **CPU and Memory Usage:**
  Whether your server resources are becoming bottlenecks.

- **Database Query Time:**
  Often the hidden source of API slowness.

How to Monitor Your APIs

1. Manual Monitoring (During Development)

Tools like Postman, curl, or browser DevTools show:

- Response time,

- Status codes.

This is fine for local testing.

2. Basic Logging

Add simple logs to your API:

Example in Flask:

python
CopyEdit
```python
import time

@app.before_request
def start_timer():
    request.start_time = time.time()

@app.after_request
def log_response(response):
    duration = time.time() - request.start_time
    app.logger.info(f"{request.method} {request.path} completed in {duration:.4f}s")
    return response
```

Example in Express:

javascript
CopyEdit
```javascript
app.use((req, res, next) => {
  const start = Date.now();
  res.on('finish', () => {
    const duration = Date.now() - start;
    console.log(`${req.method} ${req.originalUrl} took ${duration}ms`);
  });
  next();
});
```

■ Even simple logs reveal performance hotspots fast.

3. Using Professional Monitoring Tools

For production APIs, use dedicated monitoring platforms:

- **New Relic,**

- **Datadog,**

- **Elastic APM,**

- **Prometheus + Grafana.**

They provide:

- Detailed charts,

- Alerting systems,

- Historical performance trends.

Monitoring isn't optional at scale — it's survival.

Chapter 11: Documentation and Publishing Best Practices

11.1 Introduction to OpenAPI and Swagger

You've spent time carefully designing, building, and securing your API.
Now it's time to **document** it — professionally.

No matter how well your API works internally, if others (even your future self) can't easily understand how to use it, it won't succeed.

Good documentation is as important as good code.

And when it comes to documenting APIs, **OpenAPI** and **Swagger** have become the global standards.

What is OpenAPI?

OpenAPI (formerly called Swagger Specification) is a **standardized format** for describing APIs.

Think of OpenAPI as a **blueprint**:

- It defines your API endpoints,

- Describes expected inputs and outputs,

- Lists authentication methods,

- Defines error responses,

- All in a machine-readable (and human-readable) format — typically a .yaml or .json file.

Why OpenAPI Matters

- **Consistency:**
  Everyone understands the same structure and meaning.

- **Automation:**
  Tools can auto-generate API documentation, mock servers, and even client SDKs from your OpenAPI spec.

- **Developer Experience:**
  New developers can immediately understand how to interact with your API without endless back-and-forth questions.

- **Future Proofing:**
  As your API grows, maintaining a single OpenAPI document makes updates easier and safer.

What is Swagger?

Swagger originally referred to both:

- A **specification** (which is now called OpenAPI),

- And a **set of tools** for working with APIs.

Today, "Swagger" usually refers to the tooling — including:

- **Swagger Editor** (write OpenAPI specs),

- **Swagger UI** (generate beautiful interactive docs),

- **Swagger Codegen** (generate server/client code automatically).

When you hear developers say "Swagger docs," they typically mean **Swagger UI generated from an OpenAPI spec**.

Summary:

> OpenAPI defines the **standard**.
> Swagger provides the **tools** to build and visualize that standard.

Both are essential for creating professional-grade API documentation.

11.2 Documenting Your API with Swagger UI

Swagger UI is a tool that generates **beautiful, interactive documentation** from your OpenAPI spec automatically.

Instead of hand-writing clumsy text files or explaining APIs in meetings, you can simply point users to a live Swagger page where they can:

- Read about endpoints,

- See request/response examples,

- Try live API calls (if authorized).

Here's how you can set it up.

Step 1: Create Your OpenAPI Specification

You can manually write an OpenAPI .yaml or .json file.

Here's a **simple OpenAPI example** in YAML:

```
yaml
CopyEdit
openapi: 3.0.0
info:
  title: User API
  version: 1.0.0
paths:
  /users:
    get:
      summary: Get all users
      responses:
```

```yaml
'200':
  description: A list of users
  content:
    application/json:
      schema:
        type: array
        items:
          type: object
          properties:
            id:
              type: integer
            name:
              type: string
post:
  summary: Create a new user
  requestBody:
    required: true
    content:
      application/json:
        schema:
          type: object
          properties:
            name:
              type: string
  responses:
    '201':
      description: User created
```

■ This defines:

- GET /users to fetch users,

- POST /users to create a new user.

161

Step 2: Install Swagger UI

If you want Swagger UI in your local project:

In Node.js (Express example):

```bash
CopyEdit
npm install swagger-ui-express yamljs
```

In your app:

```javascript
CopyEdit
const express = require('express');
const swaggerUi = require('swagger-ui-express');
const YAML = require('yamljs');

const app = express();
const swaggerDocument = YAML.load('./openapi.yaml');

app.use('/api-docs', swaggerUi.serve, swaggerUi.setup(swaggerDocument));

app.listen(3000, () => console.log('Server running at http://localhost:3000'));
```

Now visiting http://localhost:3000/api-docs will show your interactive Swagger UI!

In Python (Flask example): Use libraries like:

- Flask-RESTX (has Swagger integration),

- Flask-Swagger-UI.

```bash
CopyEdit
pip install flask-restx
```

Example in Flask:

python
CopyEdit
```python
from flask import Flask
from flask_restx import Api

app = Flask(__name__)
api = Api(app)

@api.route('/users')
class UserList(Resource):
    def get(self):
        return [{'id': 1, 'name': 'Alice'}]

if __name__ == '__main__':
    app.run(debug=True)
```

■ Flask-RESTX automatically exposes Swagger docs at /.

Step 3: Customize and Polish

You can:

- Add authentication support (e.g., API key auth),

- Add descriptions and examples for each field,

- Group endpoints into categories (tags),

- Add error responses for clarity.

The richer your OpenAPI file, the better your Swagger documentation.

11.3 Hosting Your API Documentation Online

Once you generate beautiful Swagger documentation, you'll want to **share it publicly** — especially if you're publishing APIs for external users, customers, or even just for internal teams.

Here are your best options.

Option 1: Host Swagger UI Yourself

- Deploy your API and Swagger UI server to services like:

  - **Render.com,**

  - **Vercel,**

  - **AWS EC2,**

  - **Heroku (easy for beginners).**

Users can access your docs at:

arduino
CopyEdit
https://yourapp.com/api-docs

■ Full control over branding and access.

Option 2: Use SwaggerHub

SwaggerHub is a hosted solution by the creators of Swagger.

Advantages:

- Free for small projects,

- Collaborative (multiple users editing the same spec),

- Automatic hosting of your docs,

- Versioning support.

URL might look like:

arduino
CopyEdit
https://app.swaggerhub.com/apis/yourname/yourapi/1.0.0

■ Super quick if you don't want to maintain servers yourself.

Option 3: Publish Static Docs

You can export Swagger UI as **static HTML/CSS/JS** files and host them anywhere (e.g., GitHub Pages, Netlify, custom servers).

- Generate the Swagger static bundle,

- Upload it to your static host,

- Done.

■ Lightweight, easy to share without server-side dependencies.

Best Practices for Public API Documentation

- **Protect sensitive environments**: Never expose admin or dev APIs to public users.

- **Provide examples** for all requests and responses.

- **Keep documentation updated** when the API changes.

- **Clearly indicate API versions** (especially when deprecating old ones).

11.4 How to Publish and Share Your API on GitHub

Sharing your API publicly — or even internally for teams — often involves publishing it to **GitHub**.

Let's walk through best practices for publishing APIs there.

Step 1: Prepare Your Repository

Structure your GitHub repository neatly:

```
bash
CopyEdit
/openapi.yaml
/README.md
/app/ (your code)
```

- The OpenAPI spec (openapi.yaml) should be clearly accessible.

- Include clear README instructions:

    - What the API does,

    - How to run it locally,

    - How to authenticate,

    - Link to the live Swagger documentation if hosted.

Step 2: Push to GitHub

Create a new GitHub repo:

```
bash
CopyEdit
git init
git add .
git commit -m "Initial API commit"
git remote add origin https://github.com/yourname/yourapi.git
```

```
git push -u origin main
```

■ Now your code and documentation are publicly available.

Step 3: Enable GitHub Pages (Optional)

If you want to host static Swagger UI directly from GitHub:

- Build a static Swagger UI site,

- Push it into a gh-pages branch,

- Enable GitHub Pages in repository settings.

GitHub will give you a free link like:

arduino
CopyEdit
https://yourname.github.io/yourapi/

where users can browse your API documentation easily.

Bonus: Badges and Enhancements

- Add **badges** to your README (e.g., build status, API version).

- Use **GitHub Actions** to automatically deploy updated docs.

- Maintain a **CHANGELOG.md** to track API changes.

Professional presentation makes your API much more attractive to collaborators and users.

Chapter 12: Mini Project — Simple Blog Post API

12.1 Project Setup and Requirements

Now that you've mastered the fundamentals of API development — from building endpoints to securing, testing, and documenting them — it's time to pull everything together into a **mini project**.

In this chapter, you'll create a **Simple Blog Post API** where:

- Admin users can **create**, **read**, **update**, and **delete** blog posts,

- Anyone can **view** public posts,

- Basic authentication secures sensitive operations,

- Full CRUD (Create, Read, Update, Delete) functionality is implemented.

What We Will Build

- **POST /posts** → Create a new blog post (Admin only).

- **GET /posts** → List all blog posts (Public).

- **GET /posts/:id** → Get a single post by ID (Public).

- **PUT /posts/:id** → Update a blog post (Admin only).

- **DELETE /posts/:id** → Delete a blog post (Admin only).

Simple, clean, and fully professional.

Technologies You Can Use

You can choose between:

- **Python + Flask**,
  or

- **Node.js + Express**.

Both stacks are simple and efficient for a beginner-friendly project. (We'll show examples for both where necessary.)

Project Structure

Recommended folder structure:

```
bash
CopyEdit
/simple-blog-api
 app.py (or app.js)
 /models
   post.py (or post.js)
 /routes
   post_routes.py (or post_routes.js)
 /auth
   auth.py (or auth.js)
 openapi.yaml
 README.md
```

Keeping code modular (separating models, routes, authentication) makes it cleaner and easier to expand later.

Key Requirements

- Posts must have at least:

  - id (unique identifier),

- title (string),

- content (string),

- author (string),

- created_at (timestamp).

- Only authenticated admin users can create, update, or delete posts.

- Anyone can fetch and read posts without authentication.

- API should return appropriate HTTP status codes and error messages.

- Basic documentation should be written.

■ This will practice almost every major API development skill you've learned so far!

12.2 Building CRUD Endpoints for Posts

Let's get into the real coding — building out each CRUD endpoint.

Create a New Post — POST /posts

Admin only — Must authenticate before posting.

Request Body (JSON):

json
CopyEdit
```
{
  "title": "My First Blog Post",
  "content": "This is the body of the blog post.",
  "author": "AdminUser"
}
```

Successful Response:

- Status: 201 Created

- Body: Created post object with id and created_at timestamp.

Get All Posts — GET /posts

Public — Anyone can fetch.

Request:

bash
CopyEdit
GET /posts

Successful Response:

- Status: 200 OK

- Body: List of posts.

Example:

json
CopyEdit
```
[
  {
    "id": 1,
    "title": "First Post",
    "author": "AdminUser",
    "created_at": "2025-04-25T12:00:00Z"
  },
  ...
]
```

171

Get a Single Post by ID — GET /posts/:id

Public — Anyone can fetch.

Request:

```bash
CopyEdit
GET /posts/1
```

Response:

- Status: 200 OK with post object if found,

- 404 Not Found if post does not exist.

Update a Post — PUT /posts/:id

Admin only — Must authenticate before updating.

Request:

```json
CopyEdit
{
  "title": "Updated Blog Post",
  "content": "Updated content."
}
```

- Updates title and content fields.

- author and created_at stay the same.

Response:

- Status: 200 OK

172

- Body: Updated post object.

Delete a Post — DELETE /posts/:id

Admin only — Must authenticate before deleting.

Request:

bash
CopyEdit
DELETE /posts/1

Response:

- Status: 204 No Content if successfully deleted,

- 404 Not Found if post does not exist.

Sample In-Memory Data Storage

For simplicity (no database yet), store posts in a list:

python
CopyEdit
posts = []

or

javascript
CopyEdit
let posts = [];

Each post is just a dictionary/object added to the list.

■ Later you can easily swap in a real database when you're ready (e.g., MongoDB, SQLite).

12.3 Adding Simple Authentication for Admin Users

To secure sensitive endpoints (create, update, delete), we'll add **basic token-based authentication**.

Simple Authentication Logic

- Admin user logs in once and gets a token (hardcoded for simplicity here).

- Client sends token in the Authorization header for protected routes.

- API checks the token before allowing sensitive actions.

Example Admin Token:

nginx
CopyEdit
Bearer admin123token

Protecting Routes (Flask Example)

python
CopyEdit
```
from flask import request, abort

ADMIN_TOKEN = "admin123token"

def require_auth(func):
    def wrapper(*args, **kwargs):
        auth_header = request.headers.get('Authorization')
        if auth_header != f"Bearer {ADMIN_TOKEN}":
            abort(401, "Unauthorized access")
        return func(*args, **kwargs)
    wrapper.__name__ = func.__name__
    return wrapper

@app.route('/posts', methods=['POST'])
@require_auth
def create_post():
    ...
```

174

Protecting Routes (Express Example)

javascript
CopyEdit

```
const ADMIN_TOKEN = 'admin123token';

function requireAuth(req, res, next) {
  const auth = req.headers['authorization'];
  if (auth !== `Bearer ${ADMIN_TOKEN}`) {
    return res.status(401).json({ error: 'Unauthorized access' });
  }
  next();
}

app.post('/posts', requireAuth, (req, res) => {
  ...
});
```

■ Now, only authenticated requests with the correct token can create, update, or delete posts.

Good Practices

- Never hardcode tokens in real apps — use a proper login system later.

- Always return meaningful error responses (401 Unauthorized) if authentication fails.

12.4 Testing and Documenting the Blog API

You now have a working CRUD API secured by simple authentication.
It's time to **test** and **document** it professionally.

Testing the Blog API (Manual)

Use Postman or Thunder Client to test:

1. **GET /posts** → Should work without any headers.

2. **POST /posts** → Should **fail** without a valid Authorization token.

3. **POST /posts** (with valid token) → Should create a post.

4. **GET /posts/:id** → Should return the correct post.

5. **PUT /posts/:id** (with token) → Should update post.

6. **DELETE /posts/:id** (with token) → Should delete post.

Test both **happy paths** and **error paths** (unauthorized, not found, invalid data).

■ Catch bugs now before anyone else does.

Documenting the Blog API

You should create a basic **OpenAPI (Swagger)** spec.

At minimum, document:

- Available endpoints,

- Request body examples,

- Response examples,

- Authentication requirements.

Sample Swagger Summary:

```yaml
yaml
CopyEdit
openapi: 3.0.0
info:
  title: Simple Blog API
  version: 1.0.0
paths:
  /posts:
    get:
```

```yaml
      summary: List all posts
      responses:
       '200':
        description: List of posts
     post:
      summary: Create a post (Admin only)
      security:
       - bearerAuth: []
      requestBody:
       content:
        application/json:
         schema:
          $ref: '#/components/schemas/Post'
      responses:
       '201':
        description: Post created
 /posts/{id}:
   get:
     summary: Get post by ID
     parameters:
      - in: path
       name: id
       required: true
       schema:
        type: integer
     responses:
      '200':
        description: A single post
      '404':
        description: Not found
components:
 schemas:
   Post:
     type: object
     properties:
      title:
       type: string
      content:
       type: string
```

```
      author:
        type: string
securitySchemes:
  bearerAuth:
    type: http
    scheme: bearer
```

■ Use Swagger UI to visualize and share your documentation.

Chapter 13: Mini Project — Weather Information API

13.1 Setting Up Third-Party Weather API Integration

In this mini project, you'll build a **Weather Information API** — a useful, real-world API that fetches live weather data based on user queries.

Rather than manually collecting meteorological data (which would require massive infrastructure), you'll **integrate a third-party weather service**.
This is an essential skill for real-world API developers:

> **Learning to connect to external APIs, process their responses, and present clean, user-friendly endpoints.**

Choosing a Weather API Provider

There are many excellent weather APIs available. Popular free or freemium choices include:

- **OpenWeatherMap** (openweathermap.org),

- **WeatherAPI** (weatherapi.com),

- **Visual Crossing Weather** (visualcrossing.com).

For this project, we'll assume you're using **OpenWeatherMap**, which offers:

- Free tier (limited calls per minute),

- Simple JSON-based responses,

- City-based queries,

- Forecast data.

Setting Up Your Weather API Account

1. Go to https://openweathermap.org/.

2. Create a free account.

3. Generate an **API key**.

4. Save your API key securely — you'll need it for your backend to call the weather service.

■ Once you have your API key, you're ready to start coding.

How Weather API Calls Work

Example request to OpenWeatherMap:

```bash
CopyEdit
GET
https://api.openweathermap.org/data/2.5/weather?q=London&appid=YOUR_API_KEY
```

Query parameters:

- q: City name.

- appid: Your API key.

Response (sample):

```json
CopyEdit
{
  "weather": [{ "description": "light rain" }],
  "main": {
```

180

```
  "temp": 280.32,
  "feels_like": 278.41
 },
 "name": "London"
}
```

You'll use this data to build your own friendly Weather API for users!

13.2 Creating Endpoints for Weather Queries

Now, let's design your local Weather Information API that:

- **Receives city names** from users,

- **Fetches live weather data** from the external weather service,

- **Returns clean, simple responses.**

Project Structure

Organize your project like this:

```
bash
CopyEdit
/weather-api
 app.py (or app.js)
 /services
  weather_service.py (or weather_service.js)
 /routes
  weather_routes.py (or weather_routes.js)
 config.py (or config.js)
 README.md
```

Separation of concerns — cleanly separate your API calling logic, routes, and configurations.

Building the Endpoints

You'll build at least two key endpoints:

1. Current Weather Endpoint
bash
CopyEdit
GET /weather?city=London

- Accepts a city name via query parameter.

- Returns current weather description, temperature, feels-like temperature, and city name.

2. Forecast Endpoint (Optional Advanced)
sql
CopyEdit
GET /forecast?city=New York

- Accepts a city name.

- Returns 3-day forecast data (or more if you like).

Example API Response (Your API)

Current Weather:

json
CopyEdit
```
{
  "city": "London",
  "temperature_celsius": 17.2,
  "feels_like_celsius": 15.6,
  "description": "light rain"
}
```

182

■ Clean, minimal, and easy for frontend or app developers to use.

Example Weather Service Module

Python (weather_service.py):

```python
python
CopyEdit
import requests
import os

API_KEY = os.getenv('WEATHER_API_KEY')

def get_current_weather(city):
    url =
f"https://api.openweathermap.org/data/2.5/weather?q={city}&appid={API_KEY}&units=metric"
    response = requests.get(url)
    if response.status_code != 200:
        return None
    data = response.json()
    return {
        "city": data["name"],
        "temperature_celsius": data["main"]["temp"],
        "feels_like_celsius": data["main"]["feels_like"],
        "description": data["weather"][0]["description"]
    }
```

■ This encapsulates external API calls cleanly.

Express (weather_service.js):

```javascript
javascript
CopyEdit
const axios = require('axios');
const API_KEY = process.env.WEATHER_API_KEY;

async function getCurrentWeather(city) {
```

183

```
  const url =
`https://api.openweathermap.org/data/2.5/weather?q=${city}&appid=${API_KEY}&un
its=metric`;
  const response = await axios.get(url);
  return {
    city: response.data.name,
    temperature_celsius: response.data.main.temp,
    feels_like_celsius: response.data.main.feels_like,
    description: response.data.weather[0].description
  };
}

module.exports = { getCurrentWeather };
```

■ Clean separation allows easy maintenance or switching providers later.

13.3 Handling API Keys Securely

A critical professional practice is **never hardcoding your API keys into your source code**.

Why?

- If you accidentally upload to GitHub, your keys could be stolen.

- Keys could be misused to rack up charges or abuse your account.

How to Handle API Keys Properly

- **Use Environment Variables** to store your keys securely on your machine.

- **Access environment variables** in your code using:

    o os.getenv('KEY_NAME') **(Python),**

- process.env.KEY_NAME (Node.js).

Setting Environment Variables

In your terminal:

```bash
CopyEdit
export WEATHER_API_KEY=your_real_key
```

- Or create a local .env file (with libraries like python-dotenv or dotenv in Node.js).

■ **Pro Tip:**
Always add .env files to your .gitignore so you never accidentally commit secrets.

Good Practice Example

config.py (Python):

```python
CopyEdit
import os

WEATHER_API_KEY = os.getenv('WEATHER_API_KEY')
```

config.js (Node.js):

```javascript
CopyEdit
require('dotenv').config();
const WEATHER_API_KEY = process.env.WEATHER_API_KEY;
```

■ Your API code stays clean, and your keys stay safe.

13.4 Adding City-Based Filtering and Forecast Feature

Let's expand your Weather API by adding **city-based filtering** and a simple **forecast endpoint**.

City-Based Filtering (Already Built-In)

Since the city is passed as a query parameter:

```bash
CopyEdit
GET /weather?city=Paris
```

your API can return results for **any valid city** dynamically.

■ Done!

Adding Forecast Feature

You can also extend your API to fetch multi-day forecasts from OpenWeatherMap:

Forecast Endpoint from OpenWeatherMap:

```bash
CopyEdit
https://api.openweathermap.org/data/2.5/forecast?q=London&appid=YOUR_API_KEY
```

This API returns forecast data in 3-hour intervals over 5 days.

Building a /forecast Endpoint

Python (weather_service.py):

```python
CopyEdit
def get_forecast(city):
```

186

```python
    url =
f"https://api.openweathermap.org/data/2.5/forecast?q={city}&appid={API_KEY}&unit
s=metric"
    response = requests.get(url)
    if response.status_code != 200:
        return None
    data = response.json()
    forecast_list = []
    for entry in data['list']:
        forecast_list.append({
            "datetime": entry["dt_txt"],
            "temperature_celsius": entry["main"]["temp"],
            "description": entry["weather"][0]["description"]
        })
    return forecast_list
```

Node.js (weather_service.js):

javascript
CopyEdit

```javascript
async function getForecast(city) {
  const url =
`https://api.openweathermap.org/data/2.5/forecast?q=${city}&appid=${API_KEY}&un
its=metric`;
  const response = await axios.get(url);
  return response.data.list.map(entry => ({
    datetime: entry.dt_txt,
    temperature_celsius: entry.main.temp,
    description: entry.weather[0].description
  }));
}
```

■ Now your API supports current weather **and** detailed forecasts — amazing!

187

Chapter 14: Mini Project — User Registration and Login API

14.1 Building Secure User Registration

In this mini-project, you'll create one of the most essential and common APIs in modern applications — a **User Registration and Login API**.

Handling user accounts requires extra care because **you're dealing with sensitive personal data**.
Your approach must prioritize:

- **Security,**

- **Clarity,**

- **Scalability.**

What We Will Build

Your API will have these endpoints:

- **POST /register** → Create a new user account,

- **POST /login** → Authenticate and receive a token,

- **POST /refresh** → Get a new token with a refresh token (basic session management).

■ Clean, modern, and secure.

Required Data for Users

Every user will have at least:

- id (unique identifier),

- email (string, unique),

- password (hashed, not plain text),

- created_at (timestamp).

Project Structure Overview

Folder structure:

```bash
CopyEdit
/user-auth-api
  app.py (or app.js)
  /models
    user_model.py (or user_model.js)
  /routes
    auth_routes.py (or auth_routes.js)
  /services
    auth_service.py (or auth_service.js)
  config.py (or config.js)
  README.md
```

Separation of concerns keeps your authentication system **modular** and **secure**.

Basic Workflow

1. User sends email and password to /register.

2. API hashes the password and stores the user securely.

189

3. User sends credentials to /login.

4. API validates credentials and returns a **JWT token**.

5. User uses the token to access protected resources.

■ First, you need to accept registration requests safely.

Registration Endpoint (POST /register)

Request Example:

```json
CopyEdit
{
  "email": "user@example.com",
  "password": "securepassword123"
}
```

API must:

- Validate input (no missing or malformed data),

- Check for existing users with the same email,

- Hash the password securely,

- Store user record safely.

Response:

```json
CopyEdit
{
  "message": "User registered successfully."
}
```

Common Registration Mistakes to Avoid

- Never store plain-text passwords.

- Always validate email format.

- Check password strength (optional but recommended).

14.2 Hashing Passwords for Safe Storage

Plaintext password storage is a critical security flaw.

If you store user passwords without encryption:

- A data breach would expose every user's account,

- You could face serious legal and reputational consequences.

■ Always **hash** passwords before storing them.

What is Password Hashing?

Hashing transforms a password into a **fixed-length, irreversible** string.

Even if hackers steal your database, they cannot easily recover user passwords.

Important:

> Hashing $\neq$ Encryption.
> Encryption is reversible (with a key). Hashing is one-way.

How to Hash Passwords

Python Example (bcrypt):

```python
CopyEdit
from werkzeug.security import generate_password_hash, check_password_hash

hashed_password = generate_password_hash("securepassword123")
```

Node.js Example (bcrypt):

```javascript
CopyEdit
const bcrypt = require('bcrypt');
const hashedPassword = await bcrypt.hash('securepassword123', 10);
```

■ Always use a secure, battle-tested library like bcrypt — never write your own hashing logic.

How to Verify Passwords During Login

Python:

```python
CopyEdit
check_password_hash(hashed_password, input_password)
```

Node.js:

```javascript
CopyEdit
await bcrypt.compare(input_password, hashedPassword);
```

■ Never compare plain-text passwords manually — always use secure hash comparison functions.

192

Good Hashing Practices

- Use a strong hashing algorithm (bcrypt, argon2, pbkdf2).

- Add salt (random data) automatically (bcrypt does this).

- Never limit users to weak passwords (optional: enforce minimum length).

Password security is **not optional** — it's your users' first line of defense.

14.3 Login with Token-Based Authentication (JWT)

After registration comes **login** — the moment where you **authenticate** users and give them access to protected parts of your app.

The modern standard for login is **token-based authentication** using **JWTs (JSON Web Tokens)**.

Why Use JWTs?

- **Stateless:**
  No need to store sessions on the server — tokens contain user info securely.

- **Scalable:**
  Works perfectly across load-balanced servers, microservices, and cloud-native apps.

- **Flexible:**
  Can carry extra user information (roles, permissions) inside the token.

Login Endpoint (POST /login)

Request Example:

json
CopyEdit
{

```
  "email": "user@example.com",
  "password": "securepassword123"
}
```

Server Logic

- Look up the user by email.

- Verify the password (using hashing check).

- If correct, generate a **JWT access token**.

- Return the token to the client.

Example JWT Payload

json
CopyEdit

```
{
  "user_id": 123,
  "email": "user@example.com",
  "exp": 1710000000
}
```

Where:

- user_id → Unique user ID,

- email → User's email,

- exp → Expiration timestamp (to enforce token expiration).

How to Generate JWTs

Python (using PyJWT):

python
CopyEdit
```python
import jwt
import datetime

token = jwt.encode(
    {"user_id": 123, "exp": datetime.datetime.utcnow() + datetime.timedelta(hours=1)},
    "secret_key",
    algorithm="HS256"
)
```

Node.js (using jsonwebtoken):

javascript
CopyEdit
```javascript
const jwt = require('jsonwebtoken');

const token = jwt.sign(
  { user_id: 123 },
  'secret_key',
  { expiresIn: '1h' }
);
```

■ Always **sign** your JWTs with a secure secret key.

Response Example

json
CopyEdit
```json
{
  "access_token": "your.jwt.token.here"
}
```

195

Clients store this token (usually in localStorage, sessionStorage, or cookies) and attach it in Authorization headers:

makefile
CopyEdit
Authorization: Bearer your.jwt.token.here

This token is the user's "passport" to access protected API endpoints.

14.4 Refresh Tokens and Session Management (Intro Level)

Access tokens (JWTs) usually expire after a short time (e.g., 15 minutes, 1 hour) to reduce security risks.

But what happens when a user needs to stay logged in longer?

■ That's where **refresh tokens** come in.

What is a Refresh Token?

- A **long-lived token** (e.g., valid for days or weeks),

- Issued alongside the short-lived access token,

- Used to obtain a new access token **without forcing the user to log in again**.

Refresh Token Flow

1. User logs in → Receives access token + refresh token.

2. Access token expires → Client sends refresh token to /refresh endpoint.

3. Server verifies refresh token → Issues a new access token.

■ Smooth user experience — no need to re-enter password constantly.

Example /refresh **Endpoint**

Request:

json
CopyEdit
```
{
  "refresh_token": "long_lived_refresh_token"
}
```

Server checks the refresh token, and if valid:

- Issues a new short-lived access token,

- Optionally, issues a new refresh token.

Important Security Tips:

- Store refresh tokens securely (preferably in HTTP-only secure cookies).

- Allow users to revoke refresh tokens (logout functionality).

- Always verify the authenticity of refresh tokens.

Simple Implementation Ideas

- Maintain a list of issued refresh tokens (in a database or secure store).

- Associate refresh tokens with user sessions/devices.

- Set expiration and rotation policies.

Professional apps handle refresh tokens very carefully to balance security and usability.

Chapter 15: A Beginner's Glimpse into GraphQL and Modern Trends

15.1 What is GraphQL? Why It Matters

As you build and interact with APIs, you'll start hearing more and more about **GraphQL**.
 While REST has been the dominant approach for the last two decades, **GraphQL** offers a different — and often highly efficient — way to build APIs.

Let's break down what GraphQL is, why it matters, and why every modern API developer should at least understand its basics.

What is GraphQL?

GraphQL is a **query language** and **runtime** for APIs, developed by Facebook in 2012 and open-sourced in 2015.

At its core:

- **Clients define exactly what data they need,**

- **Servers respond with precisely that data — nothing more, nothing less.**

In other words:

> **GraphQL puts the client in control.**

Instead of hitting multiple endpoints (like in REST), a client sends a **single query** specifying exactly what it wants.

A Simple GraphQL Example

Suppose you want user information.
 In REST, you might make two separate requests:

- GET /users/123

- GET /users/123/posts

In GraphQL, you could send one query:

graphql
CopyEdit

```
{
  user(id: 123) {
    name
    email
    posts {
      title
      created_at
    }
  }
}
```

And receive:

json
CopyEdit

```
{
  "data": {
    "user": {
      "name": "Alice",
      "email": "alice@example.com",
      "posts": [
        { "title": "My First Post", "created_at": "2025-04-01" },
        { "title": "Learning APIs", "created_at": "2025-04-15" }
      ]
    }
  }
}
```

■ One request. Exactly the fields needed. No over-fetching, no under-fetching.

199

Why GraphQL Matters

- **Efficiency:** Fetch multiple resources in one call.

- **Flexibility:** Clients decide exactly what data they want.

- **Strong Typing:** APIs are strongly typed; clients know exactly what data types to expect.

- **Versionless:** You evolve APIs by adding fields — no need for /v1, /v2, etc.

- **Tooling Ecosystem:** Automatic documentation, type generation, real-time APIs via subscriptions.

While not a silver bullet, **GraphQL is a major innovation** — and is especially valuable in modern, data-rich, client-driven applications.

15.2 Key Differences Between REST and GraphQL

Understanding how GraphQL differs from REST is essential to making smart architecture decisions.

Let's compare the two side-by-side.

Feature	REST	GraphQL
Data Fetching	Multiple endpoints (one per resource)	Single endpoint with flexible queries
Over-fetching/Under-fetching	Common	Rare (client specifies needs)
API Versioning	Often necessary (/v1/ , /v2/)	Rare (add fields, don't remove)
Server-Side Control	Server defines available endpoints and responses	Client defines required data
Tooling Support	Good (Postman, Swagger, etc.)	Excellent (GraphiQL, Apollo, Relay)
Real-time Capabilities	Requires extra setup (Websockets)	Built-in with Subscriptions
Error Handling	HTTP Status Codes	Error objects in response payload
Learning Curve	Lower (simpler for beginners)	Higher (schema, queries, mutations)

Summary:

- **REST**: Simple, stable, battle-tested — great for straightforward APIs.

- **GraphQL**: Flexible, efficient — ideal for modern, complex applications with varied client needs.

Both have their place.

15.3 When to Use REST vs When to Explore GraphQL

Choosing the right tool is a hallmark of a professional developer.
Neither REST nor GraphQL is "better" universally — it depends on your project's needs.

When to Use REST

- You have **standard CRUD operations** (Create, Read, Update, Delete).

- Your data structures are **simple and stable**.

- Clients generally need **full resource representations**.

- You want **easy caching** (HTTP cache is simple with REST).

- You're building small-to-medium size systems where rapid backend control is preferred.

■ REST remains perfect for many classic applications (e.g., blog systems, e-commerce backends, admin dashboards).

When to Consider GraphQL

- Clients have **highly dynamic needs** (mobile, web, IoT apps requiring different data views).

- **Reducing network calls** is critical (e.g., mobile on slow networks).

- Your data is **highly relational** (e.g., users → posts → comments → likes).

- You need **real-time updates** (GraphQL Subscriptions are excellent).

- You want **faster API evolution** without breaking clients.

■ GraphQL shines in modern, client-heavy architectures — like social media platforms, marketplaces, SaaS applications.

Professional Tip:
 You can even combine REST and GraphQL.

- REST for core services,

- GraphQL as a flexible aggregation layer for frontend apps.

Knowing when and how to mix them is an advanced skill.

15.4 Brief Overview of Serverless APIs (AWS Lambda Example)

While you're building APIs, another major modern trend you should be aware of is **serverless architecture**.

What is Serverless?

In traditional backend development:

- You manage a server (even if it's on the cloud),

- You install, update, secure, and monitor it.

In **serverless** architecture:

- You simply write functions,

- Cloud providers (AWS, Azure, Google) **run and scale them automatically**,

- You **only pay** when your code executes.

■ No servers to manage. ■ Infinite scalability. ■ Cost-effective for low-to-medium traffic apps.

How Serverless APIs Work

1. You write small pieces of logic — called **Functions** (e.g., "CreatePost", "GetWeatherData").

2. Each function is triggered by an event (like an HTTP request).

3. Cloud providers manage everything — networking, scaling, availability.

The most famous example: **AWS Lambda**.

Simple Example: AWS Lambda + API Gateway

Imagine you want a /hello endpoint.

- You write a simple Python function:

```python
CopyEdit
def lambda_handler(event, context):
    return {
        'statusCode': 200,
        'body': 'Hello, World!'
    }
```

- Deploy it to AWS Lambda.

- Connect it to an **API Gateway**.

- Anyone calling your API endpoint gets the function's output.

■ Done. No EC2 instances, no web servers, no operating system patching.

Advantages of Serverless APIs

- **Auto-scaling:** Handles 1 or 1 million requests without extra work.

- **Cost Savings:** No charges for idle time — only pay for execution.

- **Simplified Maintenance:** Focus only on code, not infrastructure.

Limitations to Be Aware Of

- **Cold Starts:** First request after inactivity may be slow (depending on provider/language).

- **Execution Time Limits:** AWS Lambda has a maximum execution time (15 minutes).

- **Stateless:** No persistence between function executions (must use external databases or storage).

Serverless is not always the right answer — but it's a powerful option, especially for:

- Event-driven architectures,

- APIs with unpredictable or bursty traffic,

- Low-maintenance microservices.

Chapter 16: Career Tips for Aspiring API Developers

16.1 How to Showcase API Skills on Your Resume

Learning API development is an incredibly valuable technical skill — but **knowing how to present it properly** on your resume is just as important.

When hiring managers scan resumes, they're looking for:

- Real-world project experience,

- Clear demonstration of skills,

- Practical, results-oriented achievements.

Let's break down exactly how you should showcase your API skills to stand out.

1. Focus on Outcomes, Not Just Tools

Instead of saying:

> "Built REST APIs using Node.js."

Say something stronger:

> "Developed scalable REST APIs using Node.js and Express, improving data retrieval speed by 40% for a client-facing dashboard."

Emphasize the result, the technology used, and the real-world impact.

2. Highlight Real Projects

- Include mini projects you've completed (like Blog APIs, Weather APIs, Authentication APIs).

- Mention any real-world apps you contributed to (personal, freelance, open-source).

Example bullet points:

- "Designed and deployed a secure user authentication API (JWT-based) for a SaaS platform serving 1,000+ users."

- "Integrated third-party weather services into a RESTful API, improving city-based search functionality."

■ Real-world examples show you know how to move beyond theory.

3. Use Proper Technical Terminology

Professional resumes should use the right terms:

- RESTful API design,

- CRUD operations,

- Authentication (JWT, OAuth),

- OpenAPI documentation,

- API testing (Postman, automated scripts),

- Rate limiting and caching strategies,

- Third-party API integration (e.g., OpenWeatherMap, Stripe).

■ Using accurate terms shows you're fluent in API development, not just casually experimenting.

4. Resume Section Structure

Typical structure:

diff
CopyEdit

```
Technical Skills
- Languages: Python, JavaScript (Node.js)
- API Frameworks: Flask, Express
- Tools: Postman, Swagger, Git, Docker

Projects
- Simple Blog Post API (Python Flask) — Built full CRUD functionality, JWT-secured
authentication, OpenAPI documentation.

Experience
- Junior Developer Intern — Designed and implemented RESTful APIs, integrated AWS
Lambda serverless functions.
```

Keep it clean, direct, and **focused on results and skills**.

16.2 GitHub: Your Best API Portfolio Platform

If your resume gets you an interview, your **GitHub profile** can win you the job.

For API developers, GitHub acts as your:

- **Portfolio,**

- **Proof of skills,**

- **Living resume.**

Why GitHub Matters for API Developers

- Hiring managers often check your GitHub to **verify your code quality**.

- Recruiters can see **working examples** of your API projects.

- Shows **consistency**: active coding history signals passion and professionalism.

Best Practices for an API-Focused GitHub

1. Upload Your Projects

Upload projects like:

- Blog Post API,

- Weather Information API,

- User Authentication API,

- Mini E-commerce API (if you build one later).

■ Even small, well-documented projects are valuable.

2. Write Good README Files

Every project should have a README explaining:

- What the project does,

- How to run it locally,

- Sample API requests and responses,

- Technologies used.

Example README section:

markdown
CopyEdit
Simple Blog API
A secure, token-authenticated blog post API built with Flask.
- CRUD operations for posts
- JWT-based user authentication
- OpenAPI documentation

■ Good documentation shows you're organized — a critical trait for real-world development.

3. Use Meaningful Commit Messages

Instead of:

"fixed stuff"

Use:

"Refactored user authentication flow for better error handling"

■ Clear commit messages reflect attention to detail.

4. Showcase Testing and Documentation

Include:

- Postman collections,

- Swagger docs,

- API test cases,

- Instructions for authentication.

This **proves** you understand professional API practices, not just coding basics.

Bonus: Create a GitHub Portfolio Page

GitHub Pages allows you to build a simple portfolio site directly from your GitHub account.
You can highlight your best projects — ideal for linking in job applications!

16.3 Preparing for API Development Interview Questions

Technical interviews for API developers usually cover:

- Core API principles,

- Problem-solving skills,

- Understanding of security and performance.

Here's how to prepare smartly.

Common API Interview Topics

1. API Design Questions

- How would you design a user profile API?

- What's the best way to handle pagination in large datasets?

■ Practice explaining endpoints, methods, parameters, and responses clearly.

2. HTTP Concepts

- Difference between PUT and PATCH?

- What is idempotency in REST APIs?

■ Make sure you understand HTTP status codes, methods, and headers.

3. Authentication and Security

- How would you secure an API?

- How does JWT work?

- What's the difference between authentication and authorization?

■ Be ready to explain password hashing, token validation, and security best practices.

4. Performance and Scaling

- How would you make an API faster?

- What are some caching strategies for APIs?

■ Talk about caching headers, server-side caching, query optimizations, and CDN usage.

Tips for API Interviews

- **Explain clearly and confidently:** Interviewers care about communication, not just coding speed.

- **Draw diagrams if possible:** Show endpoint relationships visually.

- **Ask clarifying questions:** Good API designers think carefully about requirements before coding.

- **Demonstrate real-world thinking:** Mention scalability, security, and maintainability concerns.

Practicing a few **mock API design sessions** with a friend or mentor can make a massive difference.

16.4 Next Steps: Moving to Intermediate and Advanced API Development

Once you're comfortable building basic APIs, it's time to **level up**.

Here's how you can move from beginner to serious API engineer.

1. Learn Advanced API Security

Beyond basic authentication:

- OAuth 2.0 flows (Authorization Code, Client Credentials),

- Role-based access control (RBAC),

- Refresh tokens with automatic rotation,

- IP whitelisting, API key rotation,

- API Gateway security layers.

2. Deepen Your Understanding of Databases

- Optimize database queries for faster APIs,

- Build APIs with PostgreSQL, MongoDB, or cloud-native databases,

- Understand ORMs (Object-Relational Mapping) and raw SQL,

- Learn about indexing, query optimization, and transactions.

■ Efficient APIs depend heavily on fast, reliable databases.

3. Build Full-Stack Applications

Pair your API backend with:

- React, Vue, or Angular frontends,

- Mobile apps (React Native, Flutter),

- IoT integrations.

■ Full-stack projects make you extremely attractive in the job market.

4. Learn API Gateway and Microservices Architecture

- Understand how API Gateways (like AWS API Gateway) route and manage traffic,

- Build microservices that communicate via APIs,

- Study service discovery, load balancing, and rate limiting at scale.

5. Deploy APIs Like a Pro

Master cloud deployment:

- AWS (EC2, Lambda, Elastic Beanstalk),

- Azure, Google Cloud,

- Containerization (Docker),

- CI/CD pipelines for API deployment.

■ Knowing how to **build** + **ship** APIs puts you in elite developer territory.

APPENDICES

Appendix A: API Development Glossary

Essential Terms You Need to Know

Understanding API development deeply means becoming comfortable with common terminology. Here's a glossary of key terms every aspiring API developer must know:

API (Application Programming Interface)

A set of rules and protocols that allow one software application to interact with another. APIs enable different systems to communicate and exchange data.

REST (Representational State Transfer)

An architectural style for designing networked applications. RESTful APIs use HTTP methods and are stateless, scalable, and simple to use.

CRUD

Short for **Create, Read, Update, Delete** — the four basic operations in persistent storage systems (and fundamental to most APIs).

Endpoint

A specific URL where an API can access the resources it provides.
 Example: GET /users/1 retrieves user with ID 1.

HTTP Methods

- **GET:** Retrieve data.

- **POST:** Create a new resource.

- **PUT:** Update an existing resource.

- **PATCH:** Partially update a resource.

- **DELETE:** Remove a resource.

Status Code

A numeric code sent in HTTP responses indicating the result of a request.
Examples:

- 200 OK

- 201 Created

- 400 Bad Request

- 401 Unauthorized

- 404 Not Found

- 500 Internal Server Error

JSON (JavaScript Object Notation)

A lightweight data-interchange format widely used in APIs. Easy to read and write for
both humans and machines.

JWT (JSON Web Token)

A compact, URL-safe token format used to securely transmit information between
parties. Often used in authentication and authorization.

OpenAPI Specification

A standard for describing RESTful APIs. Enables automatic generation of
documentation, SDKs, and more.

Swagger

A set of open-source tools (like Swagger UI) that work with OpenAPI specifications to
create interactive API documentation.

Authentication vs Authorization

- **Authentication:** Verifying who a user is.

- **Authorization:** Checking what actions a user is allowed to perform.

Token-Based Authentication

An authentication method where a server issues a token (usually a JWT) after verifying a user's credentials. The client uses this token in subsequent requests.

Rate Limiting

Controlling how many API requests a user or system can make within a specified time frame, to prevent abuse or overload.

CORS (Cross-Origin Resource Sharing)

A security feature implemented by browsers to restrict web apps from making requests to a different domain than the one that served the web page.

Serverless

A cloud computing model where developers write code without managing servers. Functions (like AWS Lambda) execute in response to events.

Appendix B: Common API Interview Questions and Answers

Quick Guide for Beginners Preparing for Interviews

1. What is REST API?

Answer:
REST API is an architectural style that uses HTTP methods to access and manipulate resources. It is stateless, meaning each call from the client contains all the information needed to process the request.

2. What are the main HTTP methods used in APIs?

Answer:

- GET: Retrieve data,

- POST: Create a new resource,

- PUT: Update an entire resource,

- PATCH: Partially update a resource,

- DELETE: Remove a resource.

3. What is the difference between PUT and PATCH?

Answer:

- **PUT** replaces the entire resource.

- **PATCH** updates only specified fields within a resource.

4. What is an Idempotent Method?

Answer:
An idempotent method produces the same result no matter how many times it's called. Example: Multiple PUT requests updating a resource with the same data produce the same result.

5. What is JWT? How does it work?

Answer:
JWT (JSON Web Token) is a compact token containing claims about a user. After successful authentication, a server issues a JWT that the client sends with future requests for secure, stateless authentication.

6. What is Rate Limiting?

Answer:
Rate limiting restricts how many API requests a user or system can make over a period to prevent abuse or system overload.

7. How do you secure an API?

Answer:

- Use HTTPS for encryption,

- Implement authentication and authorization (JWT, OAuth2),

- Validate all inputs,

- Apply rate limiting,

- Monitor for unusual activity.

8. What's the difference between Authentication and Authorization?

Answer:

- **Authentication** verifies identity.

- **Authorization** controls access rights and permissions.

9. What is CORS and why is it important?

Answer:
CORS allows servers to specify which domains can access their resources. It's a critical browser security feature to prevent unauthorized cross-domain requests.

10. What is an API Gateway?

Answer:
An API Gateway acts as a front door for APIs, handling routing, security, rate limiting, and analytics for multiple API services behind it.

Appendix C: Free Tools and Resources for API Developers

List of Tools, Websites, and Communities to Accelerate Learning

Tools for API Development

- **Postman:** API testing and automation platform.

- **Swagger UI:** Interactive API documentation from OpenAPI specs.

- **Thunder Client (VS Code extension):** Lightweight API client for quick testing.

- **Insomnia:** Powerful API design and testing tool.

Hosting and Deployment

- **Render.com:** Simple cloud deployment for APIs and web services.

- **Vercel:** Perfect for hosting serverless APIs.

- **AWS Free Tier:** Learn serverless API deployment with AWS Lambda and API Gateway.

Learning Platforms

- **freeCodeCamp:** Free curriculum covering APIs and microservices.

- **Coursera (Google Backend Specialization):** Backend development and API design.

- **YouTube (Academind, Traversy Media):** Beginner to advanced API tutorials.

API Design and Documentation Tools

- **OpenAPI Generator:** Generate client libraries from OpenAPI specs.

- **Stoplight Studio:** Visual OpenAPI editor for professional API design.

- **Redoc:** Beautifully styled API documentation generator.

Communities and Forums

- **Stack Overflow:** Ask and answer technical API development questions.

- **Reddit r/webdev and r/learnprogramming:** Discuss API strategies and learn best practices.

- **Dev.to:** Articles and tutorials from professional API developers.

- **GitHub:** Explore open-source API projects and contribute.

■ Bookmark these — they will accelerate your learning journey.

Appendix D: Bonus Material Access Guide

How to Download Source Code, API Templates, and More

To support your learning, this book provides **free bonus material** including:

1. Source Code Repositories

- Download all mini-projects (Blog API, Weather API, User Authentication API) ready to run locally.

- Python (Flask) and Node.js (Express) versions available.

2. API Starter Templates

- Prebuilt API structures:

    o Basic CRUD Template,

- Secure Authentication Template,

- Third-Party API Integration Template.

You can use these templates to jumpstart your own API projects.

3. Postman Collections

- Download ready-to-use Postman Collections for all example APIs in the book.

- Test, modify, and extend easily without starting from scratch.

4. OpenAPI Specs and Swagger Docs

- Pre-written OpenAPI YAML files for all projects.

- Instantly visualize and customize API documentation.

How to Access

- Visit: **[Provided URL Here]**

- Enter your purchase confirmation email.

- Download all resources immediately.

(If URL distribution is restricted, authors can offer via GitHub or private Google Drive links.)

■ Bonus materials are provided to **help you build faster, learn smarter, and practice like a pro.**

www.ingramcontent.com/pod-product-compliance
Lightning Source LLC
LaVergne TN
LVHW051321050326
832903LV00031B/3291